CIRCLE IT ™

Cat

Word Search
Puzzle Book

150 pages of Pocket Puzzles and Facts

Volume 8p

Mark Schumacher
President of Lowry Global Media LLC

Maria Schumacher
Editor

Lowry Global Media LLC

Circle It, Cat Facts, Pocket Size, Book 2, Word Search, Puzzle Book

Copyright © by Lowry Global Media LLC.

ISBN: 978-1-938625-90-9

Contents

       (hey, it's a puzzle book not a novel)

Enjoy all of the

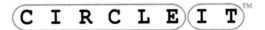

Word Search
Puzzle Books

from

LowryGlobalMedia.com

Short Stories Series:

Circle It, Snapshots, Word Search, Puzzle Book (ISBN 978-1-938625-17-6)

Circle It, Moments, Word Search, Puzzle Book (ISBN 978-1-938625-16-9)

Circle It, Anecdotes, Word Search, Puzzle Book (ISBN 978-1-938625-23-7)

Circle It, Snippets, Word Search, Puzzle Book (ISBN 978-1-938625-41-1)

Facts Series:

Circle It, Dog Facts, Book 1, Word Search, Puzzle Book (ISBN 978-1-938625-21-3)

Circle It, Cat Facts, Book 2, Word Search, Puzzle Book (ISBN 978-1-938625-25-1)

Circle It, Elk Moose & Deer Facts, Word Search, Puzzle Book (ISBN 978-1-938625-35-0)

Circle It, Bald Eagle Facts, Word Search, Puzzle Book (ISBN 978-1-938625-39-8)

Circle It, Jimmy Fallon Facts, Word Search, Puzzle Book (ISBN 978-1-938625-30-5)

Circle It, Coyote and Wolf Facts, Word Search, Puzzle Book (ISBN 978-1-938625-33-6)

Circle It, Bear Facts, Word Search, Puzzle Book (ISBN 978-1-938625-32-9)

Circle It, Trout Facts, Word Search, Puzzle Book (ISBN 978-1-938625-38-1)

Circle It, Italian Coffee Facts, Word Search, Puzzle Book (ISBN 978-1-938625-18-3)

...and many more, all available from your favorite retailer or online book seller.

Check LowryGlobalMedia.com for the latest releases!

Introduction

It is commonly said that your brain is a muscle that should be exercised to keep it strong and sharp. What better way to keep your mind stimulated than with interesting information and challenging puzzles. Why just work your way through lists of words when you can learn some interesting facts from Wikipedia and also enjoy some stimulating Circle It word search.

How to use this book:
The **bold** words from the Wikipedia text (left page) are contained within the puzzle (on the right page). Search for them in any direction: forward, backward, up, down, and diagonally; when you find the word, Circle It. If you are not sure how a word search puzzle works, ask a friend.

It has been an absolute joy creating the Circle It volumes of word search books for you. As I create each book I find myself getting lost in enjoying the fantastic Wikipedia content; it is so interesting. Admittedly, some of the words are strange and difficult, but isn't that the point in doing a word search? Stretch your mind and enjoy the challenge.

I am so grateful for you, the reader and puzzle solver, thank you!

Enjoy,

Mark Schumacher
President
Lowry Global Media LLC

American Shorthair

The **American Shorthair** (ASH) is a breed of domestic cat **believed** to be **descended** from **European** cats **brought** to North America by **early** settlers to **protect valuable cargo** from **mice** and **rats**, not a **great variety** of **mixed breeds** with short hair.[1] **According** to the Cat Fancier's Association, in 2012, it was the 7th most popular breed of cat in the United States.[2]

American Shorthair, History

When **settlers sailed** from **Europe** to **North America**, they **carried** cats on board – ships' cats – to protect the **stores** from mice.[3] Many of these cats **landed** in the **New World**, **interbred**, and **developed special characteristics** to help them **cope** with their new life and **climate**. Early in the 20th century, a **selective** breeding **program** was **established** to **develop** the best **qualities** of these cats.

The American Shorthair is a **pedigreed** cat breed, with a **strict** conformation **standard**, as set by cat fanciers of the breed and the North American cat fancier associations such as The **International Cat Association** (TICA)[3] and the Cat Fanciers Association (CFA).[4][clarification needed] The breed is **accepted** by all North American cat **registries**. **Originally** known as the Domestic Shorthair, the breed was **renamed** in 1966 to the "American Shorthair" to better **represent** its "all-American" **origins** and to **differentiate** it from other shorthaired breeds. The name "American Shorthair" also **reinforces** the fact that the breed is a pedigreed breed **distinct** from the **random**-bred non-pedigreed domestic short-haired cats in North America, which

Cat Facts, puzzle 76

```
F Q N O I T A I C O S S A M X E Z X A T E N
R B Y M T C O L A X S H O R T H A I R T U P
P X Z T D R G W D E S C E N D E D B W O V H
I R C K F E H R E I N F O R C E S A T O K P
N A T L L U V A A N N E Y W J A V H U I L B
T Z V D I F F E R E N T I A T E R E A V P Z
E F A C V M P Y L W N U E O Q Y C G L U V T
R E W O A F A E Y O Q N M R S L S Q O O B P
N X Z P L R D T D J P F L I B R E E D S P I
A G S E U B R E E I G E S G X R A F P T W C
T D P D A T S I M T G K D I T E E U S O A C
I Z H O B O I C E A L R E N A C D D Y R T G
O I B E L I E V E D N T E S X N E K W E G R
N Q S P E C I A L M R E A E T Y O T I S B E
A W E P O R U E O I E S R C D R T R O Y D G
L C T Y O N S D R C Q E E U C Z I F T R H I
A C T P N B N I I E K I R L E E Y C A H P S
N M L B R A Y S G G Q T G E E T P M T L R T
D B E N R V L T I R Q I R N P C E T Q L O R
E D R R C W V I N E W L E E I R T V E P G I
D B S A I O S N A U O A A A I D E I C D R E
P Z R A T C J C L R R U T C A T R S V H A S
Z V X O I S A T L O L Q A O X G B O E E M S
G D F R U L R N Y P D H M F A V G J C N E R
T K R B U G E H D E H S I L B A T S E C T A
P H V L X G H D V A R I E T Y I A J Z C A X
K L D L P L S T A N D A R D C K F Z C A T J
V P I S C I T S I R E T C A R A H C C U M K
```

Solutions in back of book

3

LowryGlobalMedia.com

may nevertheless **resemble** the ASH.[4] Both the American Shorthair breed and the random-bred cats from which the breed is **derived** are sometimes called "**working cats**" because they were used for controlling rodent **populations**, e.g. on ships and **farms**.

American Shorthair, Characteristics

A very **athletic** cat, the American Shorthair has a **large**, **powerfully built body**. According to the breed standard of the Cat Fanciers' Association, the American Shorthair is a true breed of working cat.

According to the CFA, American Shorthairs are low-**maintenance** cats that are generally **healthy**, easy-going, **affectionate** with owners and **social** with **strangers**. Males are **significantly** larger than females, **weighing eleven** to **fifteen** pounds when **fully grown**. **Mature** females weigh **eight** to **twelve** pounds when they **achieve** full growth at **three** to **four** years of **age**. With a **quality diet** and **plenty** of attention, **love**, and care, they can live 15 years or **longer**, and often only **require annual vaccinations**, **veterinary checkups**, and a quality diet. These cats have **solidly** built, **powerful**, and **muscular** bodies with well-**developed shoulders**, chests, and **hindquarters**.[4]

The American Shorthair is **recognized** in more than **eighty different** colors and patterns **ranging** from the brown-patched **tabby** to the blue-eyed white, the **shaded** silvers, **smokes** and **cameos** to the calico van, and many colors in between. Some even come in **deep tones** of black, brown, or other **blends** and **combinations**.

Cat Facts, puzzle 77

```
L X E Y P V S O L I D L Y B H P O F M P C T
W E S S Q S N O I T A N I B M O C X M R O W
M C Y D S M S H D V N D X Z U X E S J L P X
T P Q L R U D V F P V R Q M H D F G C A A R
L A B L E N D S O G E M U S C U L A R M U M
E Q O O G K Z R C M U Y A N N U A L R U K H
M M D V N P O W E R F U L L Y I L K P M F B
E D Y E A I G P V A C C I N A T I O N S S Y
X R M B R V X O D A V E T E R I N A R Y Y L
V P U I T T Z P L E N T Y K L I P S U G B T
U Z U T S H O U L D E R S O C I A L M A R N
V K W L A N E L R A F F E C T I O N A T E A
J U H O V M C A M E O S K V A A Q Y I H C C
Y O I A R B B T L O N G E R B T J H N L O I
F M N C G K U I K T R E O S B W S I T E G F
S S D H M E I O T B H E L J Y E E L E T N I
T D Q I K J L N R D G Y X B S L K B N I I N
Y V U E F W T S G D E R Q E M V O L A C Z G
V P A V U F D W L N A P E E G E M O N A E I
P Q R E L O E P E N E C O Q S R S R C T D S
S G T I L U L R G I G E H L U H A E E P E Z
K P E G Y R C I E I G H T E E I A L R N V M
R H R H X N N N Q N Q H Y F C V R D P C I S
D V S T E G R O W N T T I W I K E E E X R R
F I Q Y V L D O V E J I D N T F U D A D E J
Y E E L E V E N H B E P R S G H J P U I D Q
C U E T H R E E T I X Y R Y H C T K S L V C
Q F X A S O J M Z W R C B C G P P R Q X H U
```

Kitten

A **kitten** or **kitty** is a **juvenile** domesticated cat.[1] A feline litter usually consists of two to five kittens. To **survive**, kittens need the care of their mother for the **first several weeks** of their life. Kittens are **highly social** animals and spend most of their **waking hours playing** and **interacting** with **available companions**.

Kitten, Etymology

The word "kitten" derives from **Middle English *kitoun*** (*ketoun*, *kyton* etc.), which itself came from **Old French *chitoun*, *cheton***: "kitten".[1]

The young of big cats are **called cubs** rather than kittens. **Either term** may be used for the young of smaller wild felids such as **ocelots**, **caracals**, and **lynx**, but "kitten" is usually more common for these species.

Kitten, Birth and Development

A feline **litter** usually consists of two to five kittens. The **kits** are **born** after a **gestation** that lasts between 64 and 67 days, with an average length of 66 days.[2] Kittens **emerge** in a **sac** called the ***amnion*** which is **bitten off** and **eaten** by the mother cat.[3]

For the first several weeks, kittens are **unable** to **urinate** or **defecate** without being **stimulated** by their mother.[4] They are also unable to **regulate** their body **temperature** for the first three weeks, so kittens born in temperatures less than 27 °C (81 °F) can die from **hypothermia** if they are not **kept warm** by their

Cat Facts, puzzle 78

```
C Z M D M W Z Q H X W M U P F V O T M O F A
X F V T O F Z C O A K W I T F Y P W F D M I
P G N E D A M W Q X E L B A L I A V A X O M
T L R N U P O N D L C O M P A N I O N S C R
G H D C I N R V P B W S F R E N C H I F X E
Z T O R T C Y B M C J K N C A R A C A L S H
W O N U L D E T A L U M I T S W S B H R O T
A F J U R I N A T E R M Z T C U Z E E F N O
L D N P O S H B I T T E N G T H R H R U N P
M H N O I T A T S E G G L P O E T V H J Y Y
G Z O U C Y E L S O C I A L L I N S I U K H
Z I E Z J E Y K B E F P F K E B Z P E V F E
D B Y Q D N L T I O V J N V O R W L M E E A
S J P M X W H O E T H E P O W U B A K N Z X
B W S L M S W I T M T B R P F A C Y I I E H
Z F L N I A Q A G S P Y R A N M G I T L M C
K W L L D C X B K H E E V U L N N N O E V G
L D G S D G H Y F I L H R S Y I I G U T N A
X N X K L A P E R Z N Y S A F O T S N A D K
E G P W E E K S T E L G T X T N C E N A L A
N M N U O T I H C O G W I E K U A G G T I W
N C E N F Q D W U M N U K H S C R B Q I T O
O O A R F T P X B O R N L I L T E E T K T E
X G T L G I P N S J P V R A E Y T D U Z E D
C N E Y L E R E F E U O T P T H N V R A R N
Q S N J K E M S K W L N V T G E I O J M K R
D K R S M A D R T D E F E C A T E D T F Q X
X J S L E F L R O S R B A K S G G O U R L G
```

Solutions in back of book

mother.

The mother's **milk** is **very important** for the kittens' **nutrition** and **proper growth**. This milk **transfers antibodies** to the kittens, which **helps protect them** against **infectious disease**.[5] Newborn kittens are also unable to **produce concentrated urine**, and so have a very high **requirement** for **fluids**.[6]

Kittens **open their eyes** about seven to **ten days after birth**. At first, the **retina** is **poorly developed** and **vision** is **poor**. Kittens are not able to see as well as adult cats until about ten weeks after birth.[7]

Kittens **develop** very **quickly** from about two weeks of age until their seventh week. Their **coordination** and **strength improve**, they **play-fight** with their **litter-mates**, and begin to **explore** the world outside the **nest** or **den**. They learn to **wash themselves** and others as well as play **hunting** and **stalking games**, showing their **inborn ability** as predators. These **innate skills** are developed by the kittens' mother or other adult cats bringing live prey to the nest. Later, the adult cats also **demonstrate hunting techniques** for the kittens to **emulate**.[8]

As they reach three to four weeks old, the kittens are **gradually weaned** and begin to eat solid food, with weaning usually complete by six to eight weeks.[9] Kittens live primarily on solid food after weaning, but usually continue to **suckle** from time to time until **separated** from their mothers. Some mother cats will **scatter** their kittens as early as three months of age, while others continue to look after them until they **approach sexual maturity**.

The sex of kittens is usually **easy** to **determine** at birth. By six to eight weeks they are harder to sex because of the growth of fur in the genital region. The male's **urethral opening** is round,

Cat Facts, puzzle 79

```
I N S E U E M X Z W Z D Z J Y C H B A I B Z
Q E W O Y G W M E O I R G X I M T A C J L Q
F Z C O M P A N I O N S H I G S S Z P W U L
F S S A A U Q H R H J U B T G Y F K Q Q E H
R E U B I T T E N F C R R L G S P L F P P Z
E G R E M E A T E N P V F I D R E T T I L B
N U A K R J E U S B B I M L N H G J F E A I
C C R K E T O U N L C V D N I A P N M X Y R
H H N C H I T O U N M E R W C Q T G F Q I P
E G O I T M B M N N R H O B R C N E B C N Q
T T W Y O C E L O T S X Q L N I H P D Q G B
O C G Q P U L Z L V O O G H T D Q R I S S B
N F U C Y M L C D Z M V C C A L L E D R D A
L B F V H I G H L Y K S A V A I L A B L E Y
H X G K Z D E S Q P A R L A R E V E S Q F V
M H B P L D B B B T E M P E R A T U R E E B
P I G F I L V Q S T I M U L A T E D Q K C W
U X W V N E B A N W M T O T N H O U R S A L
R E B O R N K I T O U N S R E C S U E T T K
L B T J U V E N I L E R B A T C L L L S E I
O Y E E N G L I S H I E H V T D A W H L X N
K I R I A A X P W F L G I G I W C X C E A O
I L M T B W A R M T Y U L Q K G A U N K J I
T U V H L K E P T Q F L A V R D R W B C N N
S A C E E Y S E Y S W A K I N G A N T S S M
U X W R R J N V K W J T L L M A C A D R W A
Q S O C I A L X W S G E S T A T I O N L B K
C Y S W A N Q M Z P Z K U B Y T T I K R I W
```

whereas the female's is a **slit**. Another **marked difference** is the **distance between anus** and **urethral opening**, which is greater in males than in females.

Kittens are highly social animals and spend most of their waking hours **interacting** with **available** animals and playing. Play with other kittens peaks in the third or fourth month after birth, with more **solitary** hunting and stalking play **peaking** later, at about five months.[10] Kittens are **vulnerable** to harm because they like to find **dark places** to **hide**, sometimes with **fatal results** if they are not **watched carefully**.

Although domestic kittens are commonly sent to new homes at six to eight weeks of age, it has been **suggested** that being with its mother and **litter mates** from six to twelve weeks is **important** for a kitten's **social** and **behavioural development**. [10] Usually, **breeders** will not sell a kitten that is younger than twelve weeks, and in many **jurisdictions**, it is **illegal** to give away kittens younger than eight weeks old.[11]

Kitten, Health

Domestic kittens in **developed societies** are usually **vaccinated** against **common illnesses** from two to three months of age. The usual **combination vaccination protects** against Feline viral **rhinotracheitis** (FVR), Feline **calicivirus** (C), and Feline **panleukopenia** (P). This FVRCP **inoculation** is usually given at eight, twelve and sixteen weeks, and an inoculation against **rabies** may also be given at sixteen weeks. Kittens are usually spayed or neutered at **approximately** seven months of age, but kittens as young as seven weeks may be neutered (if large enough), especially in animal shelters.[12] Such early neutering does not appear to have any long-term **health risks** to

Cat Facts, puzzle 80

```
J V B WL I N WS U G G E S T E D WS V H C
F J A Y K E K V C A R E F U L L Y WK N X O
U P G C P D B N B I P E A K I N G N S WA M
I Z D G C S D U I D N P T I S N WN N V J B
M D H N N I G WZ N D O L H B S O H A G D I
A E J K Y V N V R E A L C T R I S I D E I N
F P V X T K B A V L N I X U T A L A T A F A
P O D Z WT I E T E Y K B C L A L Q D S F T
A L O O L B L M S E F I I H B A WO Q S E I
N E A L C O L S D Q D D D L Z E T V V Q R O
L V K C M A E T E A S F E H I S T I R N E N
E E V E E S G J K I R E S U L T S WO S N Y
U D N F H S A E R O S K T I WI T N E N C H
K T F Y R H L U A C K R A Q A F Z E F E E Z
O V V P S E J Z M Q S C M X D F Z B R U N W
P D I S T A N C E S I C L A I C O S K U G Q
E O E C V L V I V B R E E D E R S T P B T A
N K M H A T E J V L C A L I C I V I R U S N
I WV I C H I M P O R T A N T F O I O H O L
A X P D C T G Q M A T E S F R R B U T F L W
N E T E I H A M S Q C B P E K H H O E B I C
U B T F N Z O WN I L Z F X R Z D P C L T D
S N M E A N B E H A V I O U R A L E T F A S
L E E D T P V U L N E R A B L E B N S C R N
I E R H I N O T R A C H E I T I S I Z S Y D
T U C S O C I E T I E S T S M O N N E I S K
D B P G N I T C A R E T N I Z L Z G J S M E
Y L E T A M I X O R P P A O E H WB O R WT
```

cats, and may even be **beneficial** in male cats.[13] Kittens are commonly **wormed** against **roundworms** from about four weeks.

Kitten, Orphaned Kittens

Kittens require a **high**-**calorie** diet that contains more **protein** than the diet of adult cats.[14] **Young orphaned** kittens require cat milk every two to four hours, and they need physical stimulation to defecate and urinate.[4] Cat **milk replacement** is **manufactured** to feed to young kittens, because cow's milk does not provide all of their **necessary nutrients**.[15]

Hand-**reared** kittens tend to be **very affectionate** with humans as adults and sometimes **more dependent** on them than kittens reared by their mothers, but they can also show **volatile mood swings** and **aggression**.[16] **Depending** on the age at which they were orphaned and how long they were without their mothers, these kittens may be **severely underweight** and as such can have **health problems later** in life, such as **heart conditions**. The **compromised immune system** of orphaned kittens (from lack of antibodies found naturally in the mother's milk) can make them **especially susceptible** to **infections**, making **antibiotics** a **necessity** when caring for such kittens.

Cat Facts, puzzle 81

```
E G U Z B C H E H Y C V P X V E X P N K Y U
I Z S U Y T N Z E V A R O Z Y G O V T A Q H
Q Z W Q D N X I U Q L E Q M V Z U O E F W G
M V Y R K B C U R D O D Q L I E U L W F X X
Y L P T V K G Y E T R M S O N E B A X E V G
P N N N I N F E C T I O N S I I P T R C U Z
D J G Q X S E V E R E L Y T T M K I Z T T T
N H O R T E S F E G I S J P C T Z L X I X P
I M M U N E H E A L T H E X U B W E B O E U
K N T N B E O E C Y Z C O N D I T I O N S Q
P M F D U R X Q J E S D V M Q I X A K A P A
F S M E L B O R P U N D E R W E I G H T E Y
R Y V O C A Y U S T Q G A A P T U G I E C E
B S W R R T T J N U T R I E N T S R G R I V
U T V P E E I E S D W H Z B L Y C E H Z A N
U E Z H A L M O R E W O R M E D O S E L L L
V M D A R A A O N T S O K J N J M S A S L V
R D E N E S N I O S X G R R K N P I R F Y Z
G C P E D T U T C D X B N M L O R O T Z F V
F D E D C Y F A I I E U N I S H O N U B Q M
D W N T W O A M S B F M A L W F M I F A P B
Z H D A F U C D U U I E G K F S I G M I I A
A U E D H N T A V Y A O N E C E S S A R Y K
I W N U J G U F P Z V A T E F C E W T K A C
Q Y T B B P R O T I E N X I B R D U R W R E
N X U M I V E R Y R E P L A C E M E N T Q E
C Z P J G M D E P E N D I N G S B T Y Y A N
Z Y F I Y D N J D C J Q E Z T I X E Y I W J
```

Solutions in back of book

Arabian Mau

The **Arabian Mau** is a **formal** breed of domestic cat, developed from the **desert** cat, a short-haired **landrace native** to the **desert** of the **Arabian Peninsula**, which lives there in the **streets** and has adapted very well to the **extreme** climate. The Arabian Mau is recognized as a formal breed only by one fancier and breeder organization and cat registry, the **Germany**-based World Cat Federation (WCF). Based on one landrace, the Arabian Mau it is a **natural** breed.

It is **medium** in size, with a body **structure** that is **rather** large and firm, not **particularly slender**, and with well **developed musculature**. The legs are **comparatively** long, with oval paws.

The head **appears round**, but is **slightly longer** than **broad**. The nose is slightly **concave curved**, when **viewed** in **profile**. The **whisker pads** are **clearly pronounced**, with a **slight pinch**. The **chin** is very **firm**. The eyes are slightly oval, large and slightly **slanted**. The cat may have any **normal** cat eye colour, and there is no **relation** between the eye and coat colours. The ears are large, slightly **forward** and **sideward**-placed, high-set on the **skull**.

The tail has medium length and tapers **slightly** towards the tip.

The coat is **short** and **lying** close to the body. It has no **undercoat** and is **firm** to **touch**. It may not be **silky**, but is **noticeably** very **glossy**.

Arabian Mau, History

The desert cat has been a landrace native to **Kuwait**, **Qatar**,

Cat Facts, puzzle 82

```
D I L D E V R U C B O R C P B C H C H J J G
E E O M K F M C A L E D A D A D E S E R T K
N M P H H I D I X M J B L T U D U K A J V W
G O E O R R Y S D M R L A Y A T S E L G Y H
K N I R L M U X I F I U N F M Q B B U G B I
U M P T T E H G E O T A D L N I L N S P D S
W G R U A X V P J R G D R S A I O S N R A K
A M N I A L E E T W R R A L I C Q L I O P E
I N C C F M E T D A A A C I B U U A N N P R
T H F B L G R R W R L D E G A Q H N E O E E
T Y Q Y K E X E R D L V L H R J J T P U A D
K Y I F S N D S N D U F J T A R Y E N N R N
M N Y E O I M R L E K I O L Y V S D A C S E
G K D F S R I A Z F S Z N Y R H J E I E O L
I V H N K X M M U I D E M D O E Q U B D Y S
E I C N O R Z A N T Y S A R T E H C A L Q Y
C E U R O T X Z L V T O T O R H O T R R M H
U W O N O S I S D R R U P U S M G A A U A C
R E T U P U R C E B B E T G P I L I S R F H
Y D J C N L N E E A Y C V A E U L C L E U I
E Y F C L D T D N A U L R A C R U K L S Y N
V J T C O S E A E R B A T I C L M I Y F L O
I R E G N O L R T W T L T H A N F A M N R R
T Z W S Q J V S C I R R Y T G O O N N U A I
A J X R Z S R H V O A T U V R I F C V Y E W
N L T Q O L R E I P A R O P S D L R H T L A
O Q E U U V L U R I E T U C I Y H S M F C D
G L O S S Y P I N C H D N A T U R A L T N G
```

Saudi Arabia, and the **United Arab Emirates** for more than 1,000 years.[1] Desert cats are well adapted to the **hot**, **arid Middle Eastern environment**.[1] The variety originated (like all domestic cats) from the African wildcat, *Felis silvestris lybica*, which has lived for many **thousands** of years on the Arabian peninsula. The **wildcat** lives in desert regions near human **settlements**. As early **cities spread** more and more into the desert, the wildcat **ventured closer** and closer to humans, because there was more food and **shelter**, and **eventually** domesticated itself.*[citation needed] Today, the desert cat variety make up a **notable proportion** of the street cats of Arabian Peninsula cities, and of course many are kept as pets.*[1]

The Arabian Mau is a natural breed (a formal breed that aims to lock-in the most **defining traits** of a landrace through **selective** breeding). The breed, as such, was **initially** developed by **Petra Mueller**, **director** of the Middle East Cat Society (MECat), who had long **observed** the cats and their behavior, throughout the **region**.[1] The name "Arabian Mau" was **coined** by Mueller, who led the efforts for breed **recognition**.[1] WCF **recognizes** three coats in the breed: tabby, white, and **bicolor**[1]

The breed was recognized, as "**provisional**" status, by the Germany-based World Cat Federation (WCF) in **November** 2008, at the **International** Cat show in **Dubai**, **cleared** for WCF cat **show** competition as of **January** 2009.[1] It was the **first** new WCF breed in over 10 years.[1]

Arabian Mau, Temperament

Arabian Mau cats have very **loving temperaments**. The main **feature** of this cat breed is their **devotion**, **love** and **affection** for the owner. This cat will always be a **reliable companion** of an

Cat Facts, puzzle 83

```
C V P R O P O R T I O N E V E R T J D T K S
X S I L V E S T R I S D O B D T S W A R H N
O A Y C O M P A N I O N E T Q Z D L N E X T
H R D L H V W I T E M P E R A M E N T S B B
B I M E B O E C T P E T P G O B Q N B P H G
S T I A R T T S D W D N B I C O L O R R U D
H E D R T A F F E C T I O N M H C E S O E B
O Z D E N B E G Q E O B S E R V E D V V N G
W U L D F A A D H Q W Z O H J Y I V I I V X
D G E Y T I I U E E O H E E G H V T L S I V
O N K U R L N S M V O Y I T A N C G A I R H
F I R M T A D I E R O T G R S E I N N O O I
G E X Q X A U T N A G T I T L R T S O N N O
A G R M L P C N K G S D I E D R I L I A M L
W R N U L O A D A U Q T S O R J E F T L E P
M N T S X O F I L J K W E M N T S L A U N K
X E O E U A M U N I T E D R E G I O N E T V
N O V I P C W V X Y W Z C X N W G Q R L L V
L S E T T L E M E N T S H E L T E R E H V J
O C N C H I R E C O G N I Z E S P D T I S J
V I T C L O N E V E N T U A L L Y B N H R R
I K U E D O U G L Y B I C A Z L U F I S Z C
N A R O A E S S O I N I T I A L L Y G B R P
G D E W W S N E A C A B W A R A B M Q T H B
D U D U B A I I R N E B D I R E C T O R A X
A M U E L L E R O J D R L T B W L J C N N N
C Z W Z L P U Y G C F S V E M I R A T E S O
C P K R E B M E V O N J Z E S D A E R P S A
```

Solutions in back of book

individual that loves his cat and **cares** for it. Arabian Mau gets very well with **children** and different kinds of animals. These cats are **neat** and take care of themselves very well. They do not take **offense** of the owner, and **forgive** him all his **punishments**. They have a nice soft and **gentle purring** coming from the inside. These cats are very **quiet**; they **meow** only if they need something or want to **attract** your **attention**.

Because Arabian Mau cats used to **live** in the desert and had to **hunt** for food **themselves**, they **enjoy eating** their food and can never get **enough**. They are not **picky** when it comes to food. They like to **play** and so this breed is very **active** and **curious**. They are good hunters, **quick** and **agile**. If you let your cat out, he will **easily** catch a prey and bring it back home. These cats easily jump and **jump high**. Outdoor cats like to **walk** around their **territory** and their **house**. Males always **guard** their territory from other male cats. But they always come back home.

Arabian Mau, Health

Arabian Mau breed has good **health**. Kittens are **born strong** and healthy, as the Arabian Mau cats have a good **immune system**. From the first day kittens are very active and **movable**. In a home with **multiple** cats, a **male** and a **female** cat will always be **dominant**. Females are good **mothers**; they always **supervise** the **process** of the kittens' **growth** and **teach** their kittens. They can **feed** their kittens up to five months. The female cat always **controls** all **situations** in the **pack** of **multiple** cats. This cat needs love, attention and human **presence**. In **return** she will always be around the owner and **follow** him **everywhere**.

18

Cat Facts, puzzle 84

```
A Q E V W N E U U P Y C J S F N Z A X Q W M
V L O D K A J Y E V N T Y I C J L Y E S B I
Q Q C D H Z X R Q T F R F L H F Z A R G H B
U U U Q Z Z L X X U S E L K X I X F X T J V
M L R I Z L L H F P P T T C K G G N I K H N
T O I O C M Z Q H M Y W A N H V G G W D Y B
T L O Y N K L D G R O W T H J W T R Y E A H
P V U S T R O N G F L V P O R X U Z H U I H
M L S O B E U W N J K C A T T E N T I O N H
T Q U H I G H W H S F O Q B N A T G N X W Z
E H P S T N E M H S I N U P L A Y U I I H W
A O E C E Y D G H A V T I F K E L R R W V D
C U R M A N E I B O P R E S E N C E T N O B
H S V A S R O P V Q M O T H E R S J O R E H
T E I L I E E U P I R L B P A C K J E G J Q
L F S E L M L S G C D S N O I T A U T I S G
A M E L Y E M V G H H U N T R C Q M X J F K
E W S E T O M U E Q W I A E D N K P E P Q Q
H J D A D W P F N S A Q L L A Z E Y N U L P
X F G U A R D A A E L T P D P T F F J R S I
K O E V L U F S Y Y K L T E R R I T O R Y Q
R L N M U L T I P L E R V R R E O N Y I S N
X L T G A C T I V E Q I M G A F N C G N T K
N O L N Z L L C W A G I L E W C B E E G E S
H W E O Y I E V E R Y W H E R E T B A S M Z
Z U S H B V K D O M I N A N T Y P E E T S T
K Z T L C E O F F E N S E F N G A R E A G H
L W M R Q Y Z K P L C Q T V X V A W B I S R
```

Solutions in back of book

Arabian Mau, Grooming

Grooming is very easy, the cat does not **shed** so much. To **brush** the coat from time to time will remove dead hairs and **intensify** the **beautiful** gloss of the coat.

Standard Arabian Mau

Females are medium sized and **elegant**; however, males can be very **huge**. They have muscular bodies though females are slightly smaller. Their legs are long with **perfectly** oval paws. They have large ears. The tail has medium length with **tapering** toward the tip. The head appears to be round, but it is slightly longer than **broad** with well-defined whisker pads. Ears are large and well set. Their eyes are oval and **match** the coat color. The fur is **short** and without any undercoat; **besides** it **lying** close enough to the body. The coat should not be silky. The colors can be **different** but the most **recognized** are red, white, black, black and white, brown and brown tabby. [2]

The Arabian Mau cat breed is a natural breed, so it must reflect the **morphology** and behavioral features of the cats living on the Arabian Peninsula. The **standard** has been **drafted** on the **observation** and the **description** of **physical characteristics**, which have been found in the cats of this area average population, **originating** from the Middle East and in its **descendants**. No **prefixed model** has been **followed**.

The Arabian Mau cat is a natural breed, so it must **reflect** the morphology and behavioral features of the cats living on the Arabian Peninsula. The standard has been **drafted** on the observation and the description of physical characteristics.

Cat Facts, puzzle 85

```
R F R S T N A D N E C S E D P H G C K B P N
B T U A E N I N C F O N Y S B Q O L J Y Y J
Q A F B N B D O T V I R B N H Y S G T F V F
W U Y E E W R G P Q X Z G L F O Z O O C I J
M E I A D B X U P N P Z I I M N R J Q U K S
T Y A U K Y W N S R H X J H N H U T O R A S
N G H T X N H Q E H Z Q W J P A L A E C W U
A D U I P E D F K I A Q G U C Y T C M H X O
G O J F K Y I P H C T A M E I S O I Y S X K
E K I U B X F A P C D E O N J G T F N J P X
L Y C L E L M S L H V G G Z N N I U Y G S C
E K O D Y W E N Z K W U Z I E S Q C I E O H
F T A P E R I N G C X H Z R N B V N D P N A
I O P H G L D B W H D E E E S P B I D D H R
N A L S N H E U W C D F T N E H S A E D Y A
M V T L B O Q I D N F N E O Y E O H T D L C
H G Y N O L I F W I I X Z C B R S K O X T T
S F R G E W T T D G A I O Q B Z M N C J C E
T V Q D H I E A P L R B G R O T U Y S L E R
A G M I N L T D F I S O I L O M M H A D F I
N R O Z Q D D K U E R T O V W R C C F E R S
D F D P X R K O R S N C H M L G I A E T E T
A U E U T A G V T Y O E S C I S T B K F P I
R O L A B F A E I I T L S E Y N G X L A R C
D U F D I T R E F G K F Q H D C G Q I R S S
E V T I I E A L E Y N E P G L C A R G D P P
T G F O N D M W Q D Y R J I D V M O O X X V
H L N O B Z W H X H Z Y G O L O H P R O M M
```

Cat Anatomy

Cat Anatomy, Mouth

Cats have **highly specialized** teeth for the killing of prey and the tearing of meat. The *premolar* and *first molar*, together the *carnassial pair* are located on each side of the mouth. These teeth **efficiently function** to **shear** meat like a pair of **scissors**. While this is present in **canids**, it is highly developed in felines.

The cat's tongue has sharp spines, or *papillae*, useful for **retaining** and **ripping** flesh from a **carcass**. These **papillae** are small backward-facing **hooks** that contain **keratin** which also assist in their groom.

The cat's oral **structures** provide for a variety of **vocalizations** used for **communication**, including meowing, purring, hissing, growling, **squeaking**, **chirping**, **clicking**, and **grunting**.

Cats also **employ** a variety of body language: position of ears and tail, **relaxation** of whole body, **kneading** of paws, all are **indicators** of **mood**.

Cat Anatomy, Ears

Thirty-two individual muscles in each **ear** allow for a manner of **directional hearing**;[1] a cat can move each ear **independently** of the other. Because of this **mobility**, a cat can move its body in one direction and point its ears in another direction. Most cats have **straight** ears pointing **upward**. Unlike dogs, flap-eared breeds are **extremely** rare (Scottish Folds are one such **exceptional** mutation). When **angry** or **frightened**, a cat will lay back its ears to **accompany** the growling or hissing sounds it makes. Cats

Cat Facts, puzzle 86

```
D U O G L F W N Q I X D V F Y L R P Q P K R
O Z Z G K A G K O Q C V O K J Y Y S P C X J
F W U F S B D X O O F P C O R J Y I O Y T B
I N D I C A T O R S U D A D M L X U N J W P
P I P P F A L Y P N F C L I C K I N G V P M
G I D E E N R S N E F F I C I E N T L Y W B
T N Z M S P E C I A L I Z E D F V V Y R Q Q
N D F B U O U N A O D S A I Q O G G P B E C
M E D C P F U L P S N X T W T K Z Q Y C I C
Y P A P I L L A E H S Z I R Q G J N I P E W
S E F K F O S Y C N X P O I U P W A R D P B
Q N I U X A C C O M P A N Y S C K S P X S W
C D I R E C T I O N A L S R F L T Q N S P F
Q E G R U N T I N G G N O S W T X U Q O I Q
K N F G E C S K T L W S G K Q H Y E R K Z C
F T Y R N T A K U C S T G R I G Y A I E U O
P L B U I V A N O I A K A W Y I P K P R S M
T Y F Q O G H I C O I N B L Y A O I P A S M
E O A R F E H S N H H Z I M I R B N I T S U
H X H X A N A T F I I O M D M T L G N I Z N
R H T R P N M R E C N R Q B S S L X G N U I
R Z I R P H Y R M N C G P R E M O L A R P C
I N L G E R S E X C E P T I O N A L G H V A
G O I J H M N H K C H D M K N E A D I N G T
I O S W T L E Y E M P L O Y W G N Y P L F I
F N I S U A Y L C A R N A S S I A L H P A O
S M O B I L I T Y G R E L A X A T I O N Z N
D G X T I D K U T W H Z Q X D P K H Y X G M
```

also turn their ears back when they are **playing** or to **listen** to a sound coming from **behind** them. The angle of cats' ears is an **important clue** to their mood.[citation needed]

Cat Anatomy, Nose

Cats are highly territorial and **secreting odors** plays a major role in cat **communication**. The nose helps cats to **identify** territories, other cats and **mates**, to **locate** food, and for **various** other **causes**.[2] A cat's sense of smell is believed to be about **fourteen** times **stronger** than that of humans. The **rhinarium** (the **leathery** bit of nose we see) is quite **tough** to allow it to **absorb** rather **rough treatment** sometimes. The color **varies** according to the genotype (**genetic makeup**) of the cat. Cat's skin has the same color as the fur but the color of the nose leather is probably **dictated** by a **dedicated** gene. Cats with **white** fur have skin **susceptible** to **damage** by **ultraviolet light** that may cause cancer. Extra care is **required** when she/he goes **outside** in hot sun.[3]

Cat Anatomy, Legs

Cats, like dogs, are **digitigrades**. They walk **directly** on their toes, with the bones of their feet making up the lower part of the **visible** leg.[4] Cats are **capable** of **walking** very **precisely**. Like all felines, they directly **register**; that is, they place each hind paw (almost) directly in the print of the **corresponding** forepaw, minimizing noise and visible tracks. This also **provides** sure **footing** for their hind paws when they **navigate** rough **terrain**. The two back legs allow **falling** and **leaping** far **distances**

Cat Facts, puzzle 87

```
O W M S T C L I C I O T N E M T A E R T T W
V A R I E S U S C E P T I B L E B R G E J J
P L A Y I N G H Y V I Z U P E Y W I C L C R
F K M U I R A N I H R D R R H E R G B F O
J I Z V H T Z S P T E E E E D E I N N A C X
V N S S D N I U F J C G H N L Y L N I P J O
N G C S T B E U P I I T F S T A E P D A B X
O E Z X L K I K S S A M O D Y I A O N C T B
I N V E A A J E T E D Z K U J E F L O L Y W
T E X M I B L E L C H T Q R G C H Y P E N J
A T Y T D Y R S W H I T E Z N H U V S X Q V
C I T H R E Q U I R E D O K H L F B E A U J
I C N Q O D D E T A T C I D K X O G R A F M
N C T N U F L I S T E N H O E X O S R R M A
U W T L G T O O C U I K S P S Q T S O N U W
M B G F H W Q U S A O D O R S B I Y C K N O
M A V Z O S E C R E T I N G U R N Y A D W E
O U T S I D E R F T D E R A N O G I U I S T
C K K E S F E A M L E A D A P S F H S S Y A
H L S G S T L U B P G E R I V B J I E T H G
V I U Z Q L R R C E E P N G R A R A S A G I
A G S E I M P O R T A N T F I E U A V N A V
L H U N S P Z G N I P A E L J T C Y W C Q A
G T G D F D A M A G E T A C O L I T Z E V N
K U L T R A V I O L E T D L H H C G L S G C
F V F W U E B V K P P R O V I D E S I Y W L
T S H H N Z Z R S K D C C R J D A Q U D B D
L M W Y I Z P U Q K H G S E B K B X T A Q G
```

without **injury**.

Unlike most mammals, when cats walk, they use a "pacing" **gait**; that is, they move the two legs on one side of the body before the legs on the other side. This **trait** is **shared** with **camels** and **giraffes**. As a walk **speeds** up into a **trot**, a cat's gait will change to be a "**diagonal**" gait, similar to that of most other mammals: the **diagonally opposite** hind and forelegs will move **simultaneously**.[5]

Cat Anatomy, Claws

Like **nearly** all members of the family Felidae, cats have **retractable** claws. In their normal, **relaxed position**, the claws are **sheathed** with the skin and fur around the toe pads. This keeps the claws **sharp** by **preventing** wear from **contact** with the ground and allows the **silent stalking** of prey. The claws on the forefeet are **typically sharper** than those on the hind feet.[6] Cats can **voluntarily extend** their claws on one or more paws. They may extend their claws in **hunting** or self-**defense**, **climbing**, "**kneading**", or for extra **traction** on soft **surfaces** (**bedspreads**, **thick rugs**, skin, etc.). It is also **possible** to make a **cooperative** cat extend its claws by **carefully pressing** both the top and bottom of the paw. The **curved** claws can become **entangled** in **carpet** or thick **fabric**, which can cause **injury** if the cat is unable to free itself.

Most cats have five claws on their front paws, and four or five on their rear paws.[7] Because of an **ancient mutation**, however, domestic and feral cats are **prone** to **polydactylyism** (**particularly** in the east coast of Canada and northeast coast of the United States), with six or seven toes.

Cat Facts, puzzle 88

```
I Y L I R A T N U L O V E Q S G U R B B W D
F N Y Z D K Z R E P R A H S E C A F R U S I
A O J L M E Y L R A L U C I T R A P W D G K
B N U U T G L Z B I G Y P S D Z Q Y H N C Q
R P C G R S P G S E K B K O M E R W I V Q P
I Z N I G Y I O N X D W Y Y S U R K L X H R
C U R V E D N L S A L S U X J I L A L S W E
R N R T Z N Z T E S T H P N O A T C H W P S
D J O D D C T G H N I N I R T D E I R S Y S
I I Y I Y L R A E N T B E S E K J Y O J L I
A S A Y T R A I T T E E L H Z A L B L N L N
G S A G Z A F U T I A G T E L L D W C M U G
O F X L O Y T S T F V A Y E A V N S S H F I
N Y K R P N L U M N E D D C S G I I H T E R
A T M W Y E A L M H T S I N Z N Y Q A O R A
L K L L M G T L S R E P O L F L E N R P A F
L H O A T I Y G T T Y T P O Y S F F P W C F
Y Q C O N T A C T T C C Y T R J P F E T O E
L G N I B M I L C F O K C E L H L E O D P S
C O O P E R A T I V E A T Q G T L I E P P G
K N E A D I N G Z K D R W N X V I B O D O N
D G X B L E W U W Y A G K R E L A X E D S I
S I T G M K N O L C A R P E T K F A K L I T
Q W E O T U Z O T R A C T I O N M Q D A T N
N O N J R Q P A R P J T U K K C I H T R E U
Q X D Z J T B W T P T B Q R N K J L M Z D H
T E Q H T L O V G N I T N E V E R P D M O V
N H N Y E H S I M U L T A N E O U S L Y F W
```

Solutions in back of book

Cat Anatomy, Temperature and Heart Rate

The normal body **temperature** of a cat is between 38 and 39 °C (101 and 102.2 °F).[8] A cat is **considered** *febrile* (**hyperthermic**) if it has a temperature of 39.5 °C (103 °F) or greater, or *hypothermic* if less than 37.5 °C (100 °F). For **comparison**, humans have a **normal** temperature of **approximately** 36.8 °C (98.6 °F). A domestic cat's normal **heart rate ranges** from 140 to 220 **beats** per minute, and is largely **dependent** on how excited the cat is. For a cat at **rest**, the average heart rate usually is between 150 and 180 bpm, about **twice** that of a human (average 80 bpm).[9]

Cat Anatomy, Skin

Cats **possess** rather **loose skin**; this allows them to turn and **confront** a **predator** or another cat in a **fight**, even when it has a grip on them. This is also an **advantage** for **veterinary purposes**, as it **simplifies injections**.[10] In fact, the lives of cats with **kidney failure** can sometimes be **extended** for years by the **regular injection** of large **volumes** of **fluid subcutaneously**, which serves as an **alternative** to **dialysis**.[11][12]

The **particularly** loose skin at the back of the neck is known as the *scruff*, and is the area by which a **mother** cat grips her kittens to **carry** them. As a result, cats tend to become **quiet** and **passive** when **gripped** there. This behavior also **extends** into **adulthood**, when a male will grab the female by the scruff to **immobilize** her while he **mounts**, and to **prevent** her from **running** away as the **mating process** takes place.[13]

This **technique** can be useful when **attempting** to **treat** or move

Cat Facts, puzzle 89

```
K P B Z P W Y P K K A Y L S N B I Y V L B Y
T T F M W M V I L Q M X S U B E X M L P X C
F L U Q O Y C V I V X E R B G H O M O A T A
I U K K V Y M W W A D F N C O N F R O N T S
C W D P F D O G V I K O C U D F A N S N I Y
T T Z P A P P R O X I M A T E L Y C E F R T
D T T D I R R I L Z D O R A P T S T A E B X
H X E J L E O P U U N T R N E G L M D B X A
W G C U U D C P M W E H Y E N Q T C V R K D
Z A H V R A E E E A Y E X O D I E O A I R U
P Y N G E T S D S Q A R G U E X A N N L S L
O U I E H O S K I N U U V S N T Z S T E I T
A D Q P Y R T V X H W G N L T E L I A L M H
L P U R P O S E S L Q E S Y A N T D G H P O
T A E E O U C T E M P E R A T U R E E X L O
E R X V T W R E L Q U I E T A W U R E X I D
R T T E H A U R A T E D S Q C T Z E I U F X
N I E N E T F I N J E C T I O N S D M I I E
A C N T R T F N O R M A L R M A T I N G E Y
T U D W M E P A S S I V E A P O S S E S S H
I L S I I M I R A N G E S R A O F L U I D A
V A R C C P H Y P E R T H E R M I C F S R G
E R S E X T E N D E D M N G I O G T L Y G M
D L Z J F I A R U J K S I U S U H G X L O W
S Y Z H Z N R U N N I N G L O N T R E A T T
M B D U W G T A M Y K H V A N T P H G I K E
E Z I L I B O M M I F P A R Y S B V I D T W
Z R T Z N H N Q C T D P Y U G M L B O U E Z
```

an **uncooperative** cat. However, since an adult cat is **heavier** than a kitten, a pet cat should never be **carried** by the scruff, but should instead have its **weight supported** at the **rump** and hind legs, and at the **chest** and front paws.[*original research?*]

Cat Anatomy, Skeleton

Cats have seven **cervical vertebrae** like almost all mammals, thirteen **thoracic** vertebrae (humans have twelve), seven **lumbar** vertebrae(humans have five), three **sacral** vertebrae (humans have five because of their **bipedal posture**), and, except for **Manx** cats and other shorter tailed cats, **twenty**-two or twenty-three **caudal** vertebrae (humans have three to five, fused into an internal coccyx). The **extra** lumbar and thoracic vertebrae account for the cat's **enhanced spinal mobility** and **flexibility**, **compared** to humans. The caudal vertebrae form the *tail*, used by the cat as a **counterbalance** to the body during **quick movements**.

Unlike human **arms**, cat **forelimbs** are **attached** to the shoulder by free-**floating clavicle** bones, which allow them to **pass** their body through any **space** into which they can fit their heads.[14]

Cat Anatomy, Skull

The cat skull is **unusual** among mammals in **having** very large eye **sockets** and a **powerful** and **specialized** jaw.[15]:35 Compared to other felines, domestic cats have **narrowly** spaced canine teeth, **adapted** to their **preferred** prey of small rodents.[16]

Cat anatomy, internal abdominal oblique muscles

This muscle's **origin** is the **lumbodorsal fascia** and **ribs**. Its **insertion** is at the **pubis** and linea alba (via **aponeurosis**), and

Cat Facts, puzzle 90

```
M V A K O R S L W F A S C I A V I J P R T M
B W N V V L P F L O A T I N G H Y K S R J U
Y F D Y Y H H M C R U M P Z M M I M V K X Y
N I F I N T K V V E R T E B R A E D D F Y F
Q Y J K S P I N A L W D O E N W R E J D Y Z
N M R G J O E L C I V A L C V J H Q F J E Y
R A X W S S R F I M G A I G W C E X T R A T
C P X B S T J D R B W F P B A X A G S I D I
E O J D A U F F W S I O Q T R E V E L B T L
R N U M B R P C J U H X T B M U I E C S T I
V E W N O E O P D W A A E U S K E J D W H B
I U S H T V W R O L U R V L Q N R E V D O O
C R P V W E E E I R X Y Z I F R I C E M R M
A O E X E Z R M I G T J X N N R P Z N P A U
L S D A N Q F B E G I E M P R G I B H T C N
C I P X T N U G A N H N D A O L E U A J I C
Z S A A Y B L I B L T T C N A L X B N S C O
X O S W C X U N C J A S Z I M A Z H C I O O
D C S H F E M S B K L N C K A U Q Y E B O P
L K H F Z R B E I X P E C N D S Y Y D U B E
U E D E R T O R P U P B B E C U E D I P C R
B T S V S T D T E S A C R A L N F Q U O A A
Q S E S T T O I D I G D N R F U E B M W U T
H G U L N W R O A D A P T E D G R P A X D I
S K T P T Y S N L L U H A F O X A P N E A V
M C B P G N A R R O W L Y Z M R S P X H L E
W U F A W Q L U M B A R P R E F E R R E D V
N Y I Y F P T F P K E I G D A M D Y W R S J
```

its **action** is the **compression** of abdominal **contents**. It also **laterally flexes** and **rotates** the vertebral **column**.

Cat Anatomy, Transversus Abdominis Muscles

This muscle is the **innermost** abdominal muscle. Its origin is the second **sheet** of the lumbodorsal fascia and the **pelvic girdle** and its insertion is the **linea alba**. Its action is the compression of the abdomen.

Cat Anatomy, Rectus Abdominis Muscles

To see this muscle, first **remove** the **extensive aponeurosis situated** on the **ventral surface** of the cat. Its **fibers** are **extremely longitudinal**, on each side of the linea alba. It is also **traversed** by the **inscriptiones tendinae**, or what others called *myosepta*.

Cat Anatomy, Deltoid Muscles

The **deltoid** muscles lie just lateral to the **trapezius** muscles, originating from several fibers spanning the clavicle and scapula, **converging** to insert at the **humerus. Anatomically**, there are only two deltoids in the cat, the *acromiodeltoid* and the *spinodeltoid*. However, to **conform** to human anatomy standards, the **clavobrachialis** is now also considered a deltoid and is commonly referred to as the *clavodeltoid*.

Cat Anatomy, Acromiodeltoid Muscles

The **acromiodeltoid** is the **shortest** of the deltoid muscles. It lies lateral to (to the side of) the **clavodeltoid**, and in a more **husky** cat it can only be seen by **lifting** or **reflecting** the clavodeltoid. It originates at the acromion process and inserts at

Cat Facts, puzzle 91

```
D F S U R E M U H L O N G I T U D I N A L S
I D O U C C R I N N E R M O S T R Z N T N I
O P A C R O M I O D E L T O I D Z Y H B X L
T E C Q F F N H R W E X T E N S I V E I N A
L L F H C L A V O D E L T O I D L C A G N I
E V I X A H A C E M R O F N O C M Q U W M H
D I B F K P L T E R M Y S B F O S S U H P C
O C E M T A O I E G G R I Q H L O J G B D A
N D R L R I L N N R B I M C A U D T H B X R
I X S T B B N B E E A Z N W W M Z P I T G B
P R N J K G A G A U A L K G P N G N R F O O
S E U D E S R E V A R T L S E J S A X W O V
V F C O M P R E S S I O N Y F C P G H O Y A
Y L J A C T I O N R V F S K R E W N J L X L
O E V Z E V O M E R X Y H I Z V V N L I B C
B C D E T A U T I S O N P I S T E A C G X J
U T I L E R N O I L W T U T U B C X G W N P
K I O P N T R J T U I S A Y Y I E J O E A Z
O N T T D Z L C Z O S Y L T M J D G V S F U
K G L F I X I S N T M V Y O E P A O H U N A
X I E L N W R E N V M L T B H S X E S Z F X
Z R D S A M S E J G E A S I E I E A U M E E
H D S S E S T N A M N X I H U T X B J R S Z
V L Y W U N V B E A K J P U S S E X E L F A
L E I Z O M B R G L F W G S R M C N B A Q K
U P J C V F T H R M L A Q K M I O N J C L L
Y O C P I X C Z I T C L M Y O S E P T A W Y
K D B J E Z B R R K W P T L X T B S G Z R E
```

the deltoid ridge. When **contracted**, it **raises** and **rotates** the **humerus outward**.

Cat Anatomy, Spinodeltoid Muscles

A **stout** and short muscle lying **posterior** to the acromiodeltoid. It lies along the lower **border** of the scapula, and it passes through the upper arm, across the upper end of muscles of the upper arm. It originates at the spine of the scapula and inserts at the deltoid ridge. Its **action** is to raise and rotate the humerus outward.

Cat Anatomy, Masseter Head Muscles

The **Masseter** is a **great**, **powerful**, and very **thick** muscle **covered** by a **tough**, **shining fascia lying ventral** to the **zygomatic arch**, which is its origin. It inserts into the posterior half of the lateral surface of the **mandible**. Its action is the **elevation** of the mandible (closing of the jaw).

Cat Anatomy, Temporalis Head Muscles

The **temporalis** is a great mass of **mandibular** muscle, and is also covered by a tough and shiny fascia. It lies **dorsal** to the zygomatic arch and fills the temporal **fossa** of the skull. It arises from the side of the **skull** and inserts into the coronoid process of the mandible. It too, elevates the jaw.

Cat Anatomy, Integumental Muscles

The two main **integumentary** muscles of a cat are the *platysma* and the *cutaneous maximus*. The *cutaneous maximus* covers the dorsal region of the cat and allows it to **shake** its skin. The *platysma* **covers** the neck and allows the cat to **stretch** the skin

Cat Facts, puzzle 92

```
K D L F B H Z O L Z Q D D E H D T B K X R N
F Z Y F L R U Y H D V K R E R U N W V C I D
Z S Y F H U J L G X E N E O M C I S R Z D O
G N Q Q G L B X U O M A N D I B U L A R N N
D R U Q D R R G D Q M A N D I B L E Q D P V
Y C K L W N E D G E Z A S P O W E R F U L K
X P D X S Y U S G L T M T S T R E T C H A T
Z X X U M T Z A W E E C N I E X S T O U T J
P J V C R Z C M X V M O A W C T K A K U Y S
P U H R T J T E J A P V W R U O E S L L S V
G U I W T B T L B T O E N I T H M R Y K M G
P Z P N M I Z S D I R R R N A N G D I B A U
F L T W T V D J Y O A E H T N N O R N M E K
N V I L O E C R S N L D X J E Q A C G D Y C
E M V I U N G H G N I Y Z S O U T W A R D Z
Z E P B G T R U P Q S C K G U C P V E T Z O
C X Z A H R E M M A X I M U S H A K E Z A J
P F F C A A A E D E Q B K M H P D M F V C U
N Z L N A L T R Q S N G E G S O W Z R U R I
M Q Y Q R I R U O X O T H I C K F N Y P K A
E E X G C O C S Q T A M A R B S U A Q K G S
P V Y R H F O S S A A L L R U X J L L K O C
R C B T E N V J A O C T R A Y A A G L V L H
K C Q Y H D E M J F T C E I I Z Q J W E D T
A S U X N T R T K W I Z N S R N K I D R H H
L T Z D A O S O G R O I R E T S O P I W F M
H J P G W A Z K B Y N J Q S H I N I N G P P
R O I J L K C D B Z H D L K O D B E S V F T
```

Solutions in back of book

over the pectoralis major and deltoid muscles.

Cat Anatomy, Rhomboideus Neck and Back Muscles

The **Rhomboideus** is a thick, large muscle below the Trapezius muscles. It extends from the vertebral **border** of the scapula to the mid-dorsal line. Its origin is from the **neural spines** of the first four thoracic **vertebrae**, and its insertion is at the **vertebral** border of the scapula. Its action is to draw the scapula to the dorsal.

Cat Anatomy, Rhomboideus Capitis Neck and Back Muscles

The Rhomboideus **Capitis** is the most cranial of the **deeper** muscles. It is **underneath** the **Clavotrapezius**. Its origin is the **superior** nuchal line, and its insertion is at the scapula. Action draws scapula **cranially**.

Cat Anatomy, Splenius Neck and Back Muscles

The **Splenius** is the most **superficial** of all the deep muscles. It is a thin, broad sheet of muscle underneath the Clavotrapezius and **deflecting** it. It is crossed also by the Rhomboideus capitis. Its origin is the mid-dorsal line of the neck and fascia. The insertion is the superior **nuchal** line and atlas. It **raises** or turns the head.

Cat Anatomy, Serratus Ventralis Neck and Back Muscles

The **Serratus Ventralis** is exposed by **cutting** the wing-like **Latissimus Dorsi**. The said muscle is covered entirely by **adipose** tissue. The origin is from the first nine or ten **ribs** and from part of the cervical vertebrae. The insertion is the vertebral

Cat Facts, puzzle 93

```
N I O G S S U P E R I O R V Y B O Z L Q S X
L K U R R H O M B O I D E U S R O B K C P V
U L J T I F L I G I W M F S Q J C Z G M L G
X T L R E A F N H O R Z H U K R Q V F C E C
R R A F X A H V V S P T J I I L I J Y N N U
S H T B S E N I P S E S D Z H N H I Y J I V
F T I Y N R T N W R S S Z E I M E C L S U E
R A S W V Z C G O R C L I P B M V Q L G M A
E E S M D E M Y V X K J D A Z B L I A C R Z
D N I W Q E R V S G N N A R R Y J E I B H S
R R M E D L F T Z M H B Q T U U L V N C Q W
O E U D H Y I L E L F G N O R E I O A W D X
B D S S G K E O E B F L V V D S N Y R O J I
F N O I I L D X C C R S K A D O A I C S T I
N U H T S S P S S B T A I L H P W Z N U T S
W J B I Y Q R E L A S I L C S I Q A O Y H O
I N N P B B R O Z M C J N V M D H E A Z A S
Z E R A E R V I D V B J P G O A E Q E Y F C
U Z H C A R P O I K F E L C W A Z P T N W Z
Y X T T T Y N F G L Z G M A R K I A T Y E X
R K U G N I T T U C H O R B D L A H C U N H
U S M M S C N G V V N L E S H L X M T B Q Y
Q T B U Y R R U Z P L T D G K Y H K L N P N
G O R I B S Q X O X R E M V F A C Y D M V O
N U M A P Z Q L E E E H S I L A R T N E V L
E T J A O V D G V P P W X P K N E U R A L N
I O Z H K W W D E L S U P E R F I C I A L B
A O K F N M K R H X N S U X N V Z V N A M H
```

border of the scapula. It draws the scapula forward, backward, and **against** the body.

Cat Anatomy, Serratus Dorsalis Neck and Back Muscles
The **Serratus Dorsalis** is **medial** to both the scapula and the Serratus Ventralis. Its origin is via **apoeurosis following** the **length** of the mid-dorsal line, and its insertion is the dorsal portion of the last ribs. Its action is to **depress** and **retracts** the ribs during **breathing**.

Cat Anatomy, Intercostals Neck and Back Muscles
The **Intercostals** are a set of muscles **sandwiched** among the ribs. They interconnect ribs, and are therefore the **primary respiratory skeletal muscles**. They are **divided** into the *external* and the *internal subscapularis*. The origin and insertion are in the ribs. The intercostals pull the ribs **backwards** or **forwards**.

Cat Anatomy, Caudofemoralis Neck and Back Muscles
The **Caudofemoralis** is a muscle found in the pelvic **limb** and is **unique** to the felids (cats).[17] The Caudofemoralis acts to **flex** the tail laterally to its **respective** side when the pelvic limb is **bearing weight**. When the pelvic limb is **lifted** off the **ground**, **contraction** of the Caudofemoralis **causes** the limb to **abduct** and the **shank** to extend by **extending** the hip **joint**.

Cat Anatomy, Pectoantebrachialis Pectoral Muscles
Pectoantebrachialis muscle is just one-half inch wide, and is the most **superficial** in the pectoral muscles. Its origin is the **manubrium** of the **sternum**, and its insertion is in a flat **tendon**

Cat Facts, puzzle 94

```
H C Z L S S U P E R F I C I A L L I B I Y D
S M F B Q W S I R A L U P A C S B U S Z V N
F P G J A C U N J I S A N D W I C H E D B P
Z M U N R E T S R D M E S I U F D Y T L C E
R B A S V Y A V A Q Y A D W Q C B N N V T C
O K N A H S R H E K F G R U E U G L Y N R T
V G T S A N R U M V D L A Y R X E X P Y E O
L I M B L S E R U B Q A W U S R Q J R T S A
L A G A I N S T I L J I R P N C P K E I P N
O I N Q A F P E R L Y D O T P I G F S N E T
W S F R M P D N B P C E F G D N R O P T C E
I C Y T E J Q D U O S M T L I Q R L I E T B
L C F J E T H O N D J N F H E U R L R R I R
I Y A X L D X N A R O I T C E X E O A C V A
S S C U R V J E M X S A O O P N T W T O E C
W K D T D G U D H J E N P A G D R I O S J H
O E T R N O Q B O R T A F T R O A N R T E I
I L I W A W F U B R B I H R O E C G Y A W A
M E J G I W C E A E S I D S U X T V G L L L
I T I C H O K C M Z A A K B N T S C Q S E I
N A Z N D T T C A O Y R L Y D E D I V I D S
U L S J T I F T A U R L I I E N B T Y S E B
J B B J O E K C C B S A N N S D O V C M P P
G S Y N G I R O R U L E L S G I Y L B T R R
B O J Z I J N N F L D W S I S N X Z R D E X
Q D W C B M S T A K O B X N S G W U R X S C
S F U P X F Q X F L G Z A S E L C S U M S A
A V V C Y R T S D L C C Z L O O E N I B A U
```

on the fascia of the **proximal** end of the **ulna**. Its action is to draw the arm towards the chest. There is no human **equivalent**.

Cat Anatomy, Pectoralis Major Muscle
The **pectoralis major**, also called *pectoralis **superficialis***, is a **broad triangular portion** of the pectoralis muscle which is **immediately** below the **pectoantebrachialis**. It is smaller than the pectoralis minor muscle. Its origin is the sternum and **median ventral raphe**, and its insertion is at the humerus. Its action is to **draw** the arm **towards** the chest.

Cat Anatomy, Pectoralis Minor Muscle
The pectoralis **minor** muscle is larger than the Pectoralis major. However, most of its **anterior border** is covered by the pectoralis major. Its origins are **ribs** three–five, and its insertion is the coracoid process of the scapula. Its actions are the **tipping** of the scapula and the **elevation** of ribs three–five.

Cat Anatomy, Xiphihumeralis Pectoral Muscles
The most **posterior**, **flat**, **thin**, and long strip of pectoral muscle is the **Xiphihumeralis**. It is a band of **parallel fibers** that is found in felines but not in humans. Its origin is the **Xiphoid Process** of the sternum. The insertion is the humerus.

Cat Anatomy, Clavotrapezius Muscle
The most anterior of the trapezius muscles, it is also the **largest**. Its fibers run obliquely to the ventral **surface**. Its origin is the **superior nuchal** line and **median** dorsal line and its insertion is the **clavicle**. Its action is to **draw** the clavicle dorsally and towards the head.

Cat Facts, puzzle 95

```
R O K B K S I L A I C I F R E P U S F D U T
O K L R E R E I P Y T R I A N G U L A R J A
I H F O M H O R T E V C M S X K M T J Y C E
R M Q A M G U I G K Q B O R D E R E N X Q R
E E J D R A E D R A W B O Z J A P Q S X A O
T D W R Q R J R L E A L A T L A H C U N A Q
N I F S D W L O R A P P C V S L F V A K L L
A A H W S G K G R J R U W L A M I X O R P E
G N G N I P P I T B C T S D T O W A R D S L
J U I O I J O K V W V S N O P I K L V I Q E
K S Y L E T A I D E M M I E C A F R U S Z V
L Q S R E B I F M Q X H U J V P S R E I T A
F G P E C T O A N T E B R A C H I A L I S T
Q M Z A B R K S I L A R E M U H I H P I X I
C O J F C T O H T Y G K B N V T A L F R C O
S I L A R O T C E P O L T S A U K F D L R N
B B A F L T K H S R X P X N N I L V A L A N
W Q Q N Q W X M O B U X K Q Q C D V D R P N
N S N B L X B N C K I E P H P P I E O N H U
V Y O C X U I L T S V T O W A C L I M Q E I
Y L I T I M G H G B J V L R L A R M Q M G O
U I T Q P D I H E I N H A E R E K T I L H G
I P R E H N B W P R D L N G T Q I T W P W C
P N O E O Z I I G A L A E S C P W C M K T F
P O P Y I Y F A Q E E S O F M Y B N I P F U
O L B J D U X B L R T P E N D R A W Z G C C
E P S E V A S D P R O C E S S C Y M X F X W
B T Z N O T N E L A V I U Q E U H Z S T P V
```

Cat Anatomy, Acromiotrapezius Muscle
Acromiotrapezius is the **middle** trapezius muscle. It covers the dorsal and lateral surfaces of the scapula. Its origin is the **neural spines** of the cervical vertebrae and its insertion is in the **metacromion** process and fascia of the **clavotrapezius**. Its action is to draw the scapula to the dorsal, and hold the two scapula **together**.

Cat Anatomy, Spinotrapezius Muscle
Spinotrapezius, also called *thoracic trapezius*, is the most posterior of the three. It is **triangular shaped**. Posterior to the acromiotrapezius and **overlaps** latissimus dorsi on the **front**. Its origin is the neural spines of the thoracic vertebrae and its insertion is the scapular fascia. Its action is to draw the scapula to the dorsal and caudal **regions**.

Cat Anatomy, Female Genitalia
In the **female cat**, the **genitalia** include two **gonads**, the **uterus**, the **vagina**, the genital **passages** and **teats**. Together with the **vulva**, the **vagina** of cat is **involved** in **mating** and **provides** a **channel** for **newborns** during *parturition*, or **birth**. The vagina is **long** and **wide**.[18] Genital passages are the **oviducts** of the cat. They are **short, narrow**, and not **very sinuous**.[18]

Cat Anatomy, Male Genitalia
In the **male** cat, the genitalia includes the **penis**, which has a very **similar surface texture** to the **tongue**.

Cat Facts, puzzle 96

```
Q J K Y Q B B A G B Y U R E K X I V Z W Z J
T Z H B B M Y N U A T F P H N V G R N K Z J
M P J Z B L W F F R M T N J F P S X A T P S
O G G V I D F O C Z Y O O G Q Z N Z K B P Q
W C P Z W W Y O S E H P V G M D J J B U K V
N D W K Z C S F P D Q J L E E J J X P L J J
G R H Y K S U W Y H M Q I E R T C D T E X D
K A T X L G I N V O L V E D P L H G Q T V R
I Q U X E T Z U W P M X S Y H U A E B G S Z
X K N W H M E T A C R O M I O N N P R K B B
T Q W Y H O P A R T U R I T I O N H S P S N
V W X N C N A E X K V X D M E T E L L M V V
B F O K C E R O N S L O D P K X L R A D Z B
N M F S J W T G A I P V L F R V T C V S F G
A A S H N B O C R N S I E B V O B U U H O Y
A R X O J O N W R U H D N R O P V I R S R I
U V O R T R I T O O A U F E Y C Z I R E O W
Q K V T H N P G W U P C E A S E M S D T A G
O W D I O S S E E S E T L O P I Q Q J E H P
I I X R R E U E D R D S B A L X M A L E S M
M Y J D A C R O M I O T R A P E Z I U S I A
K O F C C P F R O N T T R I A N G U L A R V
L G E N I T A L I A O W O X O E O T Q A J P
P G M X C M C L D V A G I N A U N E C H R P
O Z A U H H E M A T I N G D C R A R O O W N
U T L E C T I L O N G P F A E A D U A V K H
W X E S A B C A T O N G U E Y L S S R V J Q
U I V S C N Y F T C W Z H G G A Y D B C O N
```

British Shorthair

The **British Shorthair** is a domesticated cat whose **features** make it a **popular** breed in cat shows.[1] It has been the most popular breed of cat registered by the UK's **Governing** Council of the Cat Fancy (GCCF) since 2001, when it **overtook** the Persian breed.[2]

British Shorthair, Breed Description

British Shorthairs have **dense**, **plush** coats that are often **described** as **crisp** or **cracking**, referring to the way the coat breaks over the **contours** of the cat's body. Their eyes are large, round and **widely** set and can be a **variety** of colours, though the **copper** or **gold** eyes of the British blue are the best known. Their heads are round with full, **chubby cheeks** and their bodies are large and muscular. The breed has a **broad chest** and shoulders, short legs, round paws and a plush tail with a **blunt tip**.[3]

The males of this breed are larger than the females, and the size difference between them is more easily noticed compared to other breeds. The males' average weight is 5-10 **kilograms**, **whereas** a female weighs up to 5–7 kilograms. The silver shaded variety is **generally** much smaller with females being 2.6-3.5 kilograms and males being 4.2-5 kilograms. As with many breeds, the adult males may also develop **prominent cheek jowls** that distinguish them from their female **counterparts**.[4] The typical **lifespan** of this breed is less than 10 years due to many **early deaths** due to HCM, FIP etc.[3] **optimistically** states that 14–20 years is **normal**, but without

Cat Facts, puzzle 97

```
D P L Q L A W Z Y B U W O N F Q M T R O W E
S A I V S A I D Y Q M Q Y V D V S I V K I M
K T O T G F Z T K P D Q K H Q Z Y A A K E Y
G T X R I L S P O P U L A R J O L G L C F R
Q C U N B E O S F T N Z O Y Q V E D F J O M
E V X D H H D L O Y C H E G G D D E S K L N
X Q K C M P R O M I N E N T K L I U O H N R
Z Y W H E R E A S F V S D S S B W O P D R E
O D E B C H U B B Y N S S Q R T T Z U I C Y
P E R M I E C R A C K I N G E R G S D T O D
T A Y L R A E Y C U R A A V E O J P V L U U
I T O B J O T A A E E S N V Z E N L V U N O
M H S N Q E R X W M R I O E X J O U G U T Z
I S W Y I P J O W L S X B Z S Z R S K X E E
S W X R S M A R G O L I K S V B M H R T R P
T F A W U D B U D E W U V M V P A T F D P B
I V Q O N L I F E S P A N D H A L W T K A G
C O S Y M H T H N K Y F F J X L D R N P R N
A X S K E E H C S C N K C O P P E R S I T I
L E O T K G E N E R A L L Y C G S I Q O S N
L M Y M O D K N K D S S K E B H R B A R F R
Y C O N T O U R S E U G K R O C P G U C D E
S N V H S P U S R P C P I R C Y C H E E K V
F U A D H D Z U R Y Z T T U Y G B L U N T O
M F T K E E T S M K I H I A S A K J M B U G
D E L R X A P J S S A F D E B I R C S E D V
F A T W E Y E O H I E I U J G F R R G T P F
E L O F D D O F R G Q I V L I C I B M D A S
```

reference to any **scientific study**.

British Shorthair, Physical Characteristics

The British Shorthair is a very muscular cat, with a "**square**" body shape and **thick** legs. British Shorthairs have large, **broad** heads. Their eyes **stand** out and tend to be large and round. Their relatively small ears with rounded tips are set far **apart**. They have **pert snub** noses and slightly rounded chins.[5]

British Shorthair, Varieties

British Shorthairs come in many colours and **patterns**. For many years, the more popular blue variant was common enough to have a breed name of its own: the "British Blue". It **remains** one of the most popular colours, though there is now a large variety of other colour and pattern variants **accepted** by most feline governing bodies and **associations**. These include the colours black, **blue**, **white**, **red**, **cream**, chocolate, lilac, cinnamon and fawn.

British Shorthairs can be **bred** in "self" or "**solid**", which are all one colour, as well as the **colourpoint**, tabby, shaded and bicolour patterns. All colours and patterns also come in the **tortoiseshell** pattern, which is a **combination** of red and cream with other colours.[6]

British Shorthair, Temperament

British Shorthairs are an **easygoing** breed of cat; they tend to be

Cat Facts, puzzle 98

```
Q D G X V V W W M I X M C I X T U T V R L F
N M N N F X E J W T V S E X Z L Y S E S C N
X W F Q Y I W Z H O H T C Z X O W X H Q P S
V Y Y Z D H B N A R V I T Z G M J A S B A T
M K D R U H O A D T E K C Q D E M Z R Y P I
U I J U S Z S A D O H N R K V B C A K C V G
P A V D Z T L M V I N Y E X L Z Y V Z Y H A
X V F H R Y J R O S G S A N F C S C P Y D E
T S A S K D G K R E I P M F U J W J T J C L
T Y X J O M V P X S V R L K G Y L N Q Z K V
E L P X D F O C D H X V B R S F H M D T U H
N J J P L S B I A E L J Y H I I E H J W E S
U H A B E G Q Q L L A A Z G V M M P B R S X
X A A S B T Y S O L I D U C E Y U H Q V F E
B R O H S C I E N T I F I C V B Q D T W I R
M N V E B O V H H R E M A I N S T U D Y E K
L B K S N L C K W E E A M P C C G G L H N B
M U U T Q O U I J G C T S B A E A H I X R G
N E I A B U I E A A H N T Y I R E D M D E L
S O U N G R A T X T C F E A G V T V S Y U J
C E H D C P O R A C I C F R P O R N Y O W D
C S D X K O E A E N T O E O E N I R W W H D
O Q E L S I F R D K I B N P Y F T N Y W J F
T W G S S N O N T B N B I S T C E R G B U U
Y J C P Y T S N U B J R M X R E G R M Q L L
I R H L U I R C F T U E F O X A D G X G M Y
L H M O M P C P F A Y D N G C V F E I V J N
X B X E E A A E D F E E M W T D W V Q V T X
```

safe around **children** as they will **tolerate** a fair amount of **physical interaction** and **hiss** or **scratch** very **rarely**.[7] They have a **stable character** and take well to being kept as indoor-only cats, making them ideal for **apartment living**. They are very **demanding** of **attention**, though they will let their owner know if they feel like **playing**. They often **prefer** to sit **close** to their owners rather than on them.

British Shorthairs are **wonderful** cats for people who work, as they are very **happy** to **simply laze** around the house while their owner is out. They do not get **destructive** or need other **animals** for **company**, though they do enjoy having another British Shorthair or a cat with **similar temperament** around.

They are not a very **vocal** breed but will meow to **communicate** with their owners, for example when they are **hungry** and their food is being **prepared**. Some do not mind being **cuddled**, but most prefer to keep four paws on the ground and be **patted** rather than picked up.

The breed has become a **favourite** of animal **trainers** because of its nature and **intelligence**, and in **recent** years these cats have **appeared** in **Hollywood films** and **television commercials**.[4] They can learn small **tricks**.

British Shorthair, Care

British Shorthairs do not require a lot of **grooming** as their fur does not **tangle** or **mat** easily. However, it is **recommended** that the coat be **brushed occasionally**, **especially** during **seasonal shedding**, since they may develop **hairballs** at this time. British Shorthairs can be **prone** to **obesity** when **desexed** or kept indoors, so care should be taken with their diet.[3]

Cat Facts, puzzle 99

```
Z D E R A P E R P U H A I R B A L L S K Q D
C T E C G N O I S I V E L E T O B A F T D E
F M E T H U N G R Y S K C I R T L B R Q E X
Z Y C M A X K G P B R U S H E D Q L M C M E
C T L H P C M Y R H G N I Y A L P I D J A S
S L P E A E I E T O Y K R N J W Y V C C N E
R E O I R R R N Z O O S Z S G F N I R T D D
E B B S O A A A U A L M I H Y E A N E S I V
N M W J E S R C M M L E I C D T P G C F N I
I N Q R G F L M T E M U R N A O M I O A G F
A S C R A T C H O E N O D A G L O K M V A L
R C H I L D R E N H R T C F T F C B M O U N
T Y N V O T B D A Z M A A S F E B Y E U N O
B U D W M M A I E V Q N R I A C V K N R D I
L R U M I L H N T T K I L P W F W R D I J T
F A W J Z Z H B G Z T M J R A Q E E E T I C
B H C O N Z W I O L S A Q E V P K F D E N A
H F D O N D D U S O E L P F P R O N E Y T R
U U S T V D E D C S E S P E C I A L L Y E E
J S E N E E E L C O M M E R C I A L S B L T
S I A E R R R R D S I M I L A R W U S O L N
T M S C Z A P D F D Y T I S E B O G D L I I
A P O E R E A I A U U A P A R T M E N T G F
B L N R A P Y S H P L C N L J X A M P Z E X
L Y A B E P K I W D E S T R U C T I V E N M
E D L W S A O C C A S I O N A L L Y G U C R
N O I T N E T T A G N I D D E H S T I J E T
R H A P P Y L T S H M D O O W Y L L O H V L
```

British Shorthair, Health

The two biggest **health problems** in British Shorthair breed are **Hypertrophic cardiomyopathy** (HCM) and **Hip Dysplacia** (HD). A **Danish prevalence study** with more than 300 cats,[8] Prevalence of Hypertrophic Cardiomyopathy in a **Cohort** of British Shorthair Cats in **Denmark**, showed that 20.4% of males and 2.1% of the females had HCM. On top of this 6.4% of males and 3.5% of females where **judged** to be **equivocal**. The **exact** prevalence of HD is unknown, but **judging** from the few **entries** in the **Pawpeds health program** it is high. The prevalence of PKD is also unknown, but the breeds is to a large degree **founded** on Persians, which have had a 40% PKD prevalence.[9] The prevalence flat-**chested** kitten **syndrome** is unknown, but flat chested kittens are seen.

British Shorthair, Genetic Diversity

The 2008 study The **Ascent** of Cat Breeds: Genetic **Evaluations** of Breeds and **Worldwide Random**-bred **Populations** by **Lipinski** et al. **conducted** at UC **Davis** by the team led by leading feline geneticist Dr **Leslie Lyons** found that the British shorthair has a **medium** level of genetic diversity of all the breeds studied and that this is somewhat less than the average of random bred cats.[10]

Famous British Shorthairs

- **Smokey** in E.B. White's *Stuart Little* was a British Blue, although in the film **adaptation** Smokey is a **Chartreux**.
- A British Shorthair silver tabby appears on many **packages**

Cat Facts, puzzle 100

```
Z H A M F K S L P L E S L I E T S Z Y I I I
Z V I C C A M O A S T R D E D N U O F P B R
Y P C Q B H E P A C K A G E S N C Y B L J K
H R A U B X L A M L O D U S C V H X N A E S
A O L Z S X B R Y D P V T I F T N E C S A T
L G P D P Y O J W P V U I T C F R F X C J Y
P R S P P L R Z U L D C C U I Q G F I E U C
R A Y P Y O P U W Y G F Q K Q K V H I C D H
E M D O E V A L U A T I O N S E P B V H G A
V S N X M P A O T A A H N M M O D N A R I R
A S M D A N I S H S O L N O R J A W Z A N T
L H J S Y N D R O M E W I T I K V E V C G R
E C U O P A W P E D S N R P P T E D D B F E
N T X D T V C Q U R V E C E I H A R M B L U
C D E T S E H C Y W P A L I N N Q P U J C X
E G Y H Y G M W J Y A I O K I T S F A F Q E
M E D I U M Q O H L X C M V R N R K G D H D
W T Y H T A P O Y M O I D R A C B I I N A I
A F K Y A G C O H O R T J G O J E X E G S W
N N X M H E A L T H R U L U O M N Q P S M D
L S J Y M E R Y L N D H E A L T H U O V J L
E H V R C F E Q E G O H S I V A D S C N Y R
B D E N M A R K E K E J I K W T L T M Z W O
M T I A M V Y D N T O S A P Y O T U T F G W
A K V O F X E Z M X F M L B K E X A M P R Z
Y S N O I T A L U P O P S U X W B R T A V N
I D R G Z T G W B P E C O N D U C T E D C H
F Q H G H L M R Q A O H V T C A X E P K N Q
```

Solutions in back of book

and **adverts** of **Whiskas** brand cat food.

- In Terry Pratchett's **humour**/fantasy series *Discworld*, the **Lancre Witch Nanny** Ogg's cat **Greebo** (also known as "The Terror of the **Ramtops**") is often **depicted** in art as **resembling** the British Blue.[*citation needed*]
- **Winston Churchill** (Church) from *Pet Sematary* was a British Blue.
- **Happycat** (arguably the first lolcat, and also known as the "I Can Has **Cheezburger**?" cat), a **meme** started on the Something Awful forums.
- **Toby**, a fictional cat on the ABC prime time drama *Desperate Housewives*, is a British Shorthair.
- **Arlene**, a bluish grey British shorthair, as displayed in *Garfield: The Movie*
- **Mick**, from *Kamen Rider W*, is a British Shorthair who can turn into the **Smilodon Dopant**.
- Dex-star, of the Red **Lantern** Corps, is suggested to be a blue British Shorthair.
- The **Cheshire** Cat in *Alice's Adventures in Wonderland* by Lewis Carroll is a British Shorthair.
- **Ruby** in the film **adaptation** of the memoir *Girl, Interrupted* by **Susanna Kaysen** was a British Blue.

Cat Facts, puzzle 101

```
A C C B L A S R K U I D Q N N R R L D P K O
A Y Z B P R I Z P A Y R E C W C W U K B U H
I H Q Z Z B F D C F E T Y P H I Z A D J I I
A D R P N X P D H S D F T Y I E N P Y X I V
N D S K E F O L E M N H H H S C S S O L G N
B Q K W K Z J M E I A C W M K X T H T L J R
C C H L D J B E Z L L N H D A I X E I O Z E
C K Y F P L B M B O R T G U S N O K D R N W
P Z I K I G M E U D E E A F R M O I M C E G
O F E N M D V A R O D L R O W C S I D T C G
C D G Q L H M K G N N A L T S I H H Y N A T
Q F H A G Z V Q E M O N E C N P D I I H Z G
W V H O R U N O R J W C N B V X J V L D O T
N G Q O U F N W T L I R E P M H M Y L L B O
I D J T K S I X C A T E K M I T I A T V J V
C M E U G R E E B O C R G Z O R N G J D P J
X S J N F B A W L T H Z S B G T T B S A G V
F N A N N Y O M I D O U Y B E K E S Q G G O
L K O E Q X H C T V M W M R A Z R E D G A S
D T A I W S H M Q O E I N O W J R M B J O P
X K N Y T O N R C K P S C G U E U A B L I O
R B J A S A D V E R T S R K N R P T B B N E
C C Y D P E T C F S U S A N N A T A D X S Z
E K B C P O N P S A H B Q E O J E R R K P K
Q W J J D Z D X A R Q N Y M Z X D Y U B M K
E G G A B G Q W A D E S P E R A T E N W M S
H A P P Y C A T E T A D V E N T U R E S Q J
V I V D B J S Y Z D C I Z V W I M O G M K Y
```

Abyssinian

The **Abyssinian** is a **breed** of **domesticated** cat with a **distinctive ticked coat**. There are many **stories** about its **origins**, often **revolving** around **Ethiopia**, but the actual origins are **uncertain**. The Abyssinian has **become** one of the most **popular breeds** of **shorthair** cat in the **USA**.[2]

Abyssinian, History

The **name** 'Abyssinian' **refers** to Ethiopia, but most of the stories about the origins of Abyssinians **refer** to **Egypt**. **Genetic research suggests** the breed **originated** near the **coast** of the **Indian Ocean**, where **colonists** may have **purchased animals** from **wild** animal **traders**. The breed was **developed** in **Great Britain**.

The breed is **sometimes believed** to have originated from one **Egyptian female kitten** named **Zula**, who was **taken** from a port in **Alexandria** by a British **soldier** and **brought** to **England** in 1868. This **theory** is not **established** because there is no **solid link** between Zula and the cat first **listed** as an Abyssinian in 1882.[3]

Abyssinian, Appearance

The Abyssinian has **alert**, relatively **large pointed ears**. The head is **broad** and **moderately wedge shaped**. Its eyes are **almond** shaped and colors include **gold**, **green**, **hazel** or **copper**. The paws are small and **oval**. The legs are **slender** in **proportion** to the body, with a **fine** bone **structure**. The

Cat Facts, puzzle 102

```
Z K Z E T D I S T I N C T I V E B X U N Z T
B T I L B P N R V M Y C G D S V A J X B D I
J R R A T R E A J C O R I G I N A T E D M C
N J O A K I O B I I Z D E V E L O P E D F K
T E E A D E H U K N N T E M R J U T E N U E
V R K L D E S U G X I P Z R I S F E A U E D
G S O A I S R R U H A S U U A N I M A L S E
A S D A T N W S E X T L S R L T D V S J N T
L W E D G E K H U F R Y E Y C A E I J H N A
E T H I O P I A Y I E A S R B H O L A V O C
X H S L N J G N B N C R Y E T A A D Y N R I
A E I L E Z A H K E N C O L O N I S T S E T
N O L A R G E J M U U C O A S T B O E N S S
D R B Y T V F Z T K E D C I T E N E G D E E
R Y A W I L D J D A W E L O A H J D E T A M
I E T O R I G I N S V O A O A E K L B I R O
A R S T R U C T U R E S K R G T A S P I C D
L R E V O L V I N G R L Y U S M C K R D H S
M W F S D E E R B E S E S Y E O V R O N X H
O R A L U P O P F O U N O F O Q P I P A C T
N R H I Z T I E E K G D M P D E O A O L Q C
D G K S E I R O T S G E E D I M I H R G B C
B R I T A I N A M E E R T E L O N T T N G W
P E T E N D E P A H S Z I E O C T R I E U B
A E T D O O I T L Q T B M R S E J O O U L A
S N E G Y P T G U Y S X E B O B L H N P J S
V D N X N A I T P Y G E S I E E E S N Q I U
Y A C K L S U V P D E V E I L E B U K W G V
```

Abyssinian has a **fairly** long tail, broad at the base and **tapering** to a point. The Abyssinian's nose and **chin** usually form a straight **vertical line** when viewed in **profile**. A *m*-shaped marking is **often found** in the fur on the forehead. The *m*-shaped marking, also called "**frown** lines," appears **above** the Abyssinian's eyes. They can be colored **ruddy**, (usual), **chocolate**, **sorrel** (cinnamon), **blue**, **fawn**, **lilac** or sex-linked; red, **cream** and **tortoiseshell**. Abyssinians are **medium** sized cats. They have strong, **lithe** bodies with long legs.

Abyssinian, Coat and Colors

The coat is medium-length, **dense**, and **silky** to the **touch**. The Abyssinian, and a similar long-hair breed called the Somali, have coats that are **unusual enough** to **catch attention**. These felines **owe** their **special** coat to one **dominant mutant gene** known as Ta. Each hair has a **base color** with three or four darker-colored **bands**; the hair is the lighter colour at the **root**, and the darker "**ticking**" color at the tip. This ticking is found only in the Somali, Abyssinian and **Singapura**.

The **first** cat to have its **entire genome published** was an Abyssinian named **Cinnamon**.[4]

The original Abyssinian coat colour is known as 'Usual' in the United Kingdom and as 'Ruddy' **elsewhere**. The coat has a **warm reddish**-brown base, with black ticking. The feet and the backs of the hind legs are always black.

Over the **years**, **various** other **colours** have been **developed** from this original form, but the **markings** on the coat have **remained** the same. The back of the hind legs and the pads of the paws are always darker than the rest of the coat. A **popular**

Cat Facts, puzzle 103

```
W Q V Z Z D L L E H S E S I O T R O T K J S
D H K P U B L I S H E D A I K T O D S D E J
K T L J S H L O H I Q I V U N U S U A L S R
Z Q W B U C G U P S L M L A R G S L C N G F
M O L O A U L U E Z I K L X R J A Z C H T U
E M Y S I W M P O L O C Y S Q I V P D Q V C
V E R T I C A L V N I Y I M G E O K U L Y S
V F F N T H J Y G N E C W R G N N U L R X X
D E N S E I E N N W F K C L C R I A S Q A W
P E R J K N I A B O V E M A Q R I K B J B A
M I H Z Y R M E K A Q A L B T C E Q C A S I
F H R R E O M A L H N I G T E C H A G I A G
A Z A P N R W W R S L D J P N F H S M B T N
I N A X Z E E E Y K E R S E R A G Y B I U I
R T O K Y M N D D E I W A R M O N K N V F K
L O G I B A S E D Q E N H B T E F I U O T I
Y I O W T I R O U I Q A G E P E D I M V I M
N E T T D N I A R G S F U S R E H I L O O U
E P A H V E E Z V R C H U I V E X F U E D W
R M M R E D T T N I E R F E X Z T P A M U F
I W O F S O A A T W W L L S P A F M P U L A
T F K N N N F N L A O O S L Q K V H G T I C
N A O Q E E D W L O P R X Q E E N I L A S O
E W F U A G E N E E C U F Z E K V F V N D L
V N T N N P X J D U C O B D P L I V C T T O
Q D E U W D E P L S K D H N L N V U O W A R
D X N P O P U L A R U Z S C O L O U R S C D
S R P D X H N E D H L B A D L P U I D O Z E
```

colour is **Sorrel**, which has a cinnamon (**yellowish**-brown) base, with **chocolate** brown ticking, paw pads and backs of the legs. **Blue** Abyssinians, which have become **increasingly** popular in **recent** years, have a **light beige** base colour with blue ticking, paw pads and **backs** of the legs. The **relatively** rare **Fawn** Abyssinians have a light-**cream** base colour, with **darker** cream ticking and warm dark cream pads and backs of the legs.

Silver Abyssinians are a **separate** group **among** the breed. Although this colour has been in **existence** for **decades**, it is not **recognised** by the Cat **Fanciers' Association**, the world's **largest registry** of **pedigreed** cats. In Silvers, the **undercoat** is always a **pure** silvery **white**. The **markings** include black, blue, warm dark cream and cinnamon. **Purely** Silver Abyssinians are **difficult** to breed because they sometimes have **undesirable** tan **patches** in the coat. In **addition** to this, any **spots** in the coat show up more **clearly** on a silver coat.

Rare colours include the Tortoiseshell, Red, Cream, Chocolate and **Lilac**, which are all bred on a small scale in the **Netherlands** and the United Kingdom. GCCF **Standard** of points. Chocolate and Lilac abyssinians are now full **champion status** in the UK. Champion **Crystalpaws Genevieve** became the first Chocolate Abyssinian champion in GCCF.

Abyssinian **kittens** are **born** with dark coats that **gradually lighten** as they **mature**. It usually takes several **months** for the **final** coat color to be **established**.

Abyssinian, Temperament

Abyssinians are **extroverted**, **extremely active**, **playful**, **wilful** and **intelligent**. They are usually not "lap cats", because they

Cat Facts, puzzle 104

```
K R J M H W D P E D I  G R E E D A G C D Z L
S K C A B A N L A R G E S T A N D A R D Z D
I  M R T U G R A D U A L L Y Y F D D F H R K
L J  N U W D R Y R E L A T I  V E L Y S H P K
V I  F R A R E F I  N A L R T V X X F H X V G
E A G E U H Z U T E T K Y Y F P D A A T R K
R T U H O C R L N E T H E R L A N D S T G K
E C N E T S I  X E Z K L S T S T A T U S N F
G P D Q B E I  G E I  L T N D D B F X H B O U
I  Q E G B K N H T O A E C H A M P I  O N M B
S A S P O T S T W O G W F G T R U P X I  A V
T D I  T R R E I  C I  Z F I  M A R K I  N G S Q
R D R I  N N S R L R E C O G N I  S E D K C Y
Y I  A C S H E L E W I  M L Q L V A B R B R Y
O T B O K D E K A I  N C R E A S I  N G L Y L
N I  L D N T X H R L I  G H T C F M Q E J S O
P O E U N L T V L F D S F T C P A C N Q T F
I  N S I  Y M R E Y U E E O P B Y E H E R A I
S F T E A T O K N L C P Q R G O R O V I  L C
U A A O X Z V N E Y A A U S R R C C I  Q P Z
T W B N O T E E T W D R V R E E T O E M A Q
F N L L C K R R K H E A Z R E H L L V V W P
X F I  I  U I  T E E J S T C R E L C A E F S E
W P S L A E E Z M C U E Y T Z T Y T N A W T
I  F H A E R D R N E E U M E I  A I  E A E K B
I  X E C L U X V S A L N P M E V J H H P X X
U L D C Y P R J R T S Y T G X G E H W L B H
A S S O C I  A T I  O N E T L U C I  F F I  D C
```

are usually too **preoccupied** with **exploring** and **playing**.[5] They are **popular** among breeders and owners, and can be **very successful show** cats. Not all Abyssinians are shown, however, because the color and type **standards** are very **exacting**, and because some are **shy** towards **strangers** and timid in **public**. They have **quiet, engaging voices**.

"**Abys**", as they are **affectionately referred** to by their **fans**, need a great deal of **love** and **interaction** with the **family** to keep them **happy** and can get **depressed** without **daily activity** and **attention**.[3] They **generally** get along well with other cats. Abyssinians are known for their **curiosity** and enjoy **exploring** their **surroundings**, including **heights**. They are **sensible** cats that do not take **unnecessary risks**. As one might **expect** from such an intelligent and **physically capable** breed, Abyssinians are known to be **formidable hunters**. They **adore** toys and can play for **hours** with a **favorite** ball. Some play **fetch**.

Abyssinian, Health

The Abyssinian cat is **fairly** easy to **groom**. It will need an **occasional bath** and **brushing**. It can be prone to **gingivitis**, so it will need its **teeth brushed**. **Renal amyloidosis**, a **kidney disorder**, has been seen in Abyssinians.

Abyssinian, in Popular Culture

Tibs from *One **Hundred** and One **Dalmatians*** and *101 Dalmatians II: Patch's London **Adventure*** is an Abyssinian.
Jake from *The Cat from **Outer Space***.
The possible breed of the **mysterious** cat **Cassandra** in the

Cat Facts, puzzle 105

```
D N A I E G Y P D A L M A T I A N S K I I N
E D V F X P F L C Q K Y Y X R G M K P L I R
H A O F A V O R I T E I G S L R C A S P B N
F K B B C A R R Y Y K Y D Q T F C Z F R U N
T S D M T M M T P L A Y I N G E B L P E N F
U C X G I Y I H D E R R E F E R R Z T O N E
L J O F N L D B N T I B S E N Y U I L C E T
K H C L G O A I F A I R L Y E T S D O C C F
L F C J X I B H U N T E R S R V H I U U E C
K S A R A D L U L O V E N G A G I N G P S O
A T S V W O E H E I G H T S L W N T I I S D
Z R I C O S H S A T H R S U L J G E N E A G
S A O A A I D H S C I U O C Y Q Y R G D R P
U N N P T S C Y T E R M N O K H W A I U Y L
R G A A T T S E I F R V I D M L Z C V D F F
R E L B E A F A S F A P G D R T Y T I E A K
O R U L N N H P N A M N E N I E I I T O D B
U S F E T D O T F D U E S D O X D O I F V H
N C S C I A U R A A R E N A L P I N S J E J
D Q S U O R R I C B M A T I D L S W E R N P
I V E R N D S S E N S I B L E O O P H B T S
N G C I A S T K F X F E L Y H R R U A I U A
G Q C O D L H S Z F P X T Y S I D B P C R V
S L U S O C U O T A V E R Y U N E L P Q E P
G W S I R A M P W I Z Q C X R G R I Y I O B
F Z S T E E T H O U T E R T B C I C N E G E
L C D Y B T L B U P H Y S I C A L L Y T B U
G Z A C T I V I T Y A I M C I L V W S U W F
```

Solutions in back of book

Feral Cat

A **feral** cat is a domestic cat that has **returned** to the wild. It is **distinguished** from a stray cat, which is a pet cat that has been lost or **abandoned**, while feral cats are **born** in the **wild**. The **offspring** of a stray cat can be considered feral if born in the wild.[1]

In many parts of the world, feral cats are **descendants** of domestic cats that were **left behind** by **travelers**. Cats introduced into areas in which they are not **indigenous** often **cause harm** to **local environments** by preying on local **species**. This is especially true on **islands** where feral cats have sometimes had a **substantial** and **deleterious** effect on the local **fauna**.[2]

Cats have been **blamed** for the **global extinction** of 33 species. [3]

Feral Cat, Versus Stray

The term "feral" is sometimes used to **refer** to an **animal** that does not **appear friendly** when **approached** by humans, but the term can apply to any domesticated animal without human **contact**.[1] **Hissing** and **growling** are self-defense behaviors, which, over **time**, may change as the animal (whether "feral" or "stray") begins to **trust** humans that **provide food**, **water**, and **care**.[4][5]

Feral cats that are **born** and **living outdoors**, without any human contact or care, have been shown to be **adoptable** and can be **tamed** by humans, **provided** they are **removed** from a wild environment before truly feral behaviors are **established**.

Cat Facts, puzzle 106

```
B N E N V I R O N M E N T S S M P J C F A V
E Y L D N E I R F E R A L P E F M L Y W D S
M A H E D Q C N O I T C N I T X E W G I O R
F W B Q F A U N A W I L D Z V C R N S A P E
D D S A M T R U S T P Q H D P U I T Y F T L
M E P G N A G O H L D G G K X V I A X Y A I
D L S I N D I G E N O U S H I N L R C H B N
M E S C H I O W S X K N O L G H M A C I L T
Y T A A E X R N P U H I O U C H U G C S E X
D E Y R S N H P E W B K I S T S U X N S C L
C R A E T A D Y S D S S U L E D A D L I R K
O I O W A I V A M F H H T W Z A O U K N Z W
B O R N B L M D N E F G A A G J I O M G S R
O U Q B L A M E D T G O P M N Y K K R A H A
R S L H I S L A N D S L P G M T R V X S P S
N H A A S V P J U H S G R O W L I N G G C P
V R P Y H D S M L P I C O Z V A O A P G X E
M F P W E F E A P K Z R A D D N T C L P F C
L B E B D B C W J B K E C E E A E E S G D I
R R A C Y O R C N G G F H N M P P D R E J E
R E R G L O B A L L E E E R A Y N J D P Y S
P D I T B G G W U D D R D U T I D I S A S J
X I I P T Q V S G E M V B T H G V L S D R M
D V L A M I N A V T G D K E X O D D B T R T
C O N T A C T O Y G R O B R R P L S W V U G
N R V B N O M V X E G O K P Q H Y L Z S V J
E P F N J E P X X F Q F S N V E X E N R C G
A S Q S R E L E V A R T T Y G T Y J U U H U
```

Solutions in back of book

Such behaviors are established while it is **still** a kitten being **raised** by its **mother**.[4][6]

Feral Cat, Lifespan and Survival

The **lifespan** of feral cats is **hard** to **determine accurately**, although one **study reported** a median age of 4.7 years, with a **range between** 0 and 8.3 years,[7] while another **paper referenced** a mean life span of 2–8 years.[8] By **contrast**, in **captivity**, an average **life expectancy** for male **indoor** cats at birth is 12 to 14 years,[9] with females usually **living** a year or two **longer**.

Feral Cat, History

During the **Age** of **Discovery**, **ships released rabbits** onto islands to provide a **future food source** for other **travelers**. They **eventually multiplied** out of **control** and cats were introduced to keep their **numbers**, and that of mice and rats, down. The cats **tended** to **favor** local species as they were **ecologically naive** and easier to hunt. Their numbers, too, increased **dramatically** and soon they colonised many areas and were seen as **pests**. Cats were introduced to **Tasmania** in 1804 and had become feral by the 1840s. Feral cats were **reported** on **mainland** Australia around **Sydney** in 1820.[10] It has been **suggested** that feral cats could have been introduced **accidentally** to the north-western **coast** in the 17th century from the **wrecks** of **Dutch** ships; **alternatively**, they could have **arrived earlier**, possibly around the **fifteenth** century, via **mariners** from Indonesia.[11]

Cat Facts, puzzle 107

```
T E W Y L K A B J T S A O C D I X G E I E N
B K L T Y S R E L E V A R T R G M Y B T G D
E V A I A S L T G G W R E C K S I K E Q L E
B J R V R O I W U D F E L S V M X G O Y R T
B K U I R U F E I E X P E C T A N C Y H A S
N E N T I M E E D S W O A J L I V I N G B E
E L N P V V S N E I S R S U I M E F J A B G
T O W A E B P W D A A T E D F P A H C D I G
C S D C D F A Y N R Z E D N E V Y C R X T U
P S A H C Z N R E Y A D O X O W I E S R S S
D D F R C Q E D T V I H L R A D F J A N H Z
Q M I L T P E S T S E Z B V E E O N R T D I
I E L J A N D N C I J N G N R P G E N Z C K
U V I P A M O T H E R Z T E R E O E K A L G
E S T Q S Q D C L B T A N U A Q E R L L E E
N I M A I N L A N D L C W O A T C J T T Y G
I N D O O R V G B L E J M G F L O H F E J A
M N A J Y X J Q Y D B P B I O H L G U R D C
R U P I T T D F N N U I F Y O R O Y T N K C
E M L G V L L I T S Y T E E D R G S U A J U
T B O T Z E R N S N X N C N S V I R R T H R
E E N U I E S C J C D L J H O P C E E I H A
D R G V I P C O G Y O R E A U Z A N Z V X T
Q S E L I Z L F S N J V B R R C L I E E A E
K A R H V S L I G M U T E D C L L R J L K L
T A S M A N I A E U A R V R E I Y A R Y E Y
E Z H U E O J B X D F J Y J Y E R M O N C F
Y L L A C I T A M A R D S T U D Y B A Z V F
```

Solutions in back of book

Feral Cat, Diet and Predators

Domestic and feral cats have generally been found to **eat** a very broad range of vertebrate and invertebrate prey. Preferred prey usually are small mammals, birds and **lizards**, especially those with **body weights** under 100g. Feral cats in Australia prey on a variety of wildlife. In **arid** and semi-arid environments they eat mostly **introduced** European rabbits and **house** mice. In arid environments where rabbits do not occur, **native rodents** are **taken**. In **forests** and **urbanised** areas, they eat mostly native **marsupial**, birds and **reptiles**.[11] On **Macaronesian** islands, cats prey mainly on introduced mammals but also on birds and reptiles.[12]

Feral cats may be **apex predators** in some local **ecosystems**. In others, they may be preyed on by feral dogs, **dingoes**, **coyotes**, **wolves**, **bears**, **cougars**, **leopards**, **bobcats**, **lynx**, **hyenas**, **fishers**, **crocodilians**, **snakes**, **foxes** and birds of prey. [*citation needed*]

Feral Cat, Effects on Wildlife

A recent study by the **Smithsonian Conservation Biology Institute** suggests that cats are the **top threat** to US wildlife as they were found to be **responsible** for the **deaths** of up to 3.7 billion birds and 20.7 billion mammals annually, with feral and stray cats being the worst offenders.[3] These figures were much higher than **previous studies** suggested as they found cats had **killed** more than four times the amount of birds as had been previously estimated. In the US, the American **Robin** along with **shrews**, **voles**, mice, **squirrels** and rabbits were most at risk from cat predation.[3]

Cat Facts, puzzle 108

```
C C O U L Q W L J D H H F G J R H Z X N N G
U J C R O C O D I L I A N S Z E E X S A Z J
J K P G B W B M L O F R D U V S B Z C I W V
I P X R O D E N T S B G A D I P S S T N M A
X T S O E X B I O L O G Y V J O A L U O E A
U A V Q N V S A G V A C A H Q N O D B S C Q
U J G Y A I I X F H G T W K E S I R F H O K
L C L Y U R Y O S U T P K Y Q I U O X T S F
D E S I N A B R U O W S H M S B F I A I Y L
I Y O E F I M U S S Q R Q D W L E Z F M S O
N X Q P V O N A T I V E R N L E M A J S T S
G M H V A L X S D M N A K F T H H F R Q E T
O E R N N R O E T Q Z T A K E N O O N S M X
E O D E B T D W S I J D R C Z R T Q Y K S K
S E K A N S I S L C T Y I O E A R S B G S T
P L R D E L L I K U P U U S D J U S N T G W
N A I S E N O R A C A M T E W U N K U J K H
L R P O A A M U O F D S R E O Z C D P Q U C
S A M E T S T F Q V Q P Y O M T I E B T G E
E H I U X A S H O I N U N K Q E W H D S A O
T O P P L K E L S O T I F I S H E R S T P T
O U O X U T E R B Q L S B O B C A T S F L A
Y S F O Z S I M H Z N T M O C O U G A R S F
O E B N F C R E P T I L E S R N D W T F Y Z
C B N N O I T A V R E S N O C X H Y A Q A O
K O I S A V O M M G X N E X V S Y E Y M H U
V J V S U C S W E R H S L E R R I U Q S P W
P S U T N T N O F T H D Y N C X H C S C M F
```

Solutions in back of book

The **impact** of domestic cats on wildlife is a century-old debate between **passionate** cat **lovers** and those of **conservation** and **scientific beliefs**. In a 1916 report for the **Massachusetts** State Board of **Agriculture** titled *The Domestic Cat: Bird Killer, Mouser and Destroyer of Wildlife*, noted **ornithologist Edward Howe Forbush** stated in the preface:

> **Questions regarding** the **value** or **inutility** of the domestic cat, and problems connected with limiting its more or less **unwelcome** outdoor activities, are causing much **dissension**. The discussion has reached an **acute** stage. **Medical** men, **game protectors** and bird lovers call on **legislators** to **enact restrictive laws**. Then **ardent** cat lovers **rouse** themselves for **combat**. In the **excitement** of **partisanship** many **loose** and ill-considered **statements** are made.[13]

The report **cited** *Extinct Birds*, published in 1905 by **zoologist Walter Rothschild**, who stated, "man and his **satellites**, cats, rats, dogs, and **pigs** are the **worst** and in fact the only important agents of **destruction** of the native **avifaunas** wherever they go."[14] Rothschild gave several examples of cats causing the **extermination** of some bird species on islands.

Some **farmers** and **gamekeepers** see feral cats as **vermin**. Feral cats catch and eat ground **nesting** birds such as **pheasants** and **partridge**. To protect their birds, some gamekeepers set **traps** and **shoot** feral cats as part of pest control.[*citation needed*]

Cats are the **sole threat** to some bird species, such as Townsend's **Shearwater**, **Socorro** Dove, and the **Marquesan Ground Dove**,[15] or the cause of outright extinction in other cases, **notably** the Stephens Island **Wren**.

Cat Facts, puzzle 109

```
I N U T I L I T Y P D E S T R U C T I O N Z
S Z A S F Q M D F D V D X T J P O M S O Z Z
R V E O G V W P O E P A S S I O N A T E R K
O A S C T I U S R T M M L V E Z S R N Q Z W
T G A O J G P M B I A G D U M H E Q E U E E
A R T R D O I F U C H L S O E F R U M N W X
L I E R Y N N T S E I C W M V C V E E W M T
S C L O V E R S H H Y T W U O E A S T E J E
I U L O O S E I C L R S O L E D T A A L S R
G L I Z H N M S B A I I E D R I I N T C C M
E T T R T P H A E W R G P A N S O B S O I I
L U E L A T T R L S A O A G Q S N E I M E N
R R S C O O I D I H W L U M B E H X K E N A
E E T R N N F E E E T O T S E N I C S H T T
S N S H O O T N F A X H R E E S F I Z S I I
T E A U E K K T S R O T O S R I P T R M F O
R D G C O M B A T W S I I W T O U E J P I N
I W H D T M M L V A J N X N E N P M H R C J
C A R I I A E G R T Z R O B C E N E M O M T
T R V E H R E D B E A O K I E T A N G T M K
I D G I N J T R I R G R O K T S C T C E X N
V S X Y F J O R H C M A E L A S A X E C O P
E A R F R A G L A T A M R N O C E K N T I I
F I Z G R O U N D P A L T D N G U U Q O A K
G F N J I N J N P G S S A E I U I T Q R A O
L C O F K T R F A R M E R S A N T S E S C I
Q R K I P A R T I S A N S H I P G O T P E X
N M L K V H K S T T E S U H C A S S A M L P
```

Solutions in back of book

Feral Cat, Australia

Feral cats in Australia have been **linked** to the **decline** and extinction of various native animals. They have been **shown** to cause a significant **impact** on ground nesting birds and small native mammals.[11] Feral cats have also **hampered** any attempts to re-introduce **threatened** species back into areas where they have become extinct as the cats have **simply** hunted and killed the **newly** released animals.[16] **Numerous** Australian **environmentalists claim** the feral cat has been an ecological **disaster** in Australia, **inhabiting** most ecosystems **except dense rainforest**, and being **implicated** in the extinction of several marsupial and **placental** mammal species.[17]

Feral Cat, New Zealand

The fauna of New Zealand has **evolved** in **isolation** for millions of years without the presence of mammals (apart from a few bat species). **Consequently**, birds dominated the **niches occupied** by mammals and many became **flightless**. The introduction of mammals after **settlement** by Māori from about the 12th century had a **huge** effect on the indigenous **biodiversity**. European **explorers** and **settlers** brought cats on their ships and the presence of feral cats were **recorded** from the **latter** decades of the 19th century.[18] It is estimated that feral cats have been responsible for the extinction of six **endemic** bird species and over 70 localised **subspecies** as well as **depleting** bird and **lizard** species.[19]

Cat Facts, puzzle 110

```
A A S C V T D O F Y W R E C O R D E D U G I
B D T E A Z R T S S A O Y U U X O Y N V X Y
S Q G K S E H C O B E Y U Q F Y O Y J L R Z
T O R U T L U X Y D A I R F X Z S P I W D E
S Q O T W X K K E C L C C U A S A G R K C X
I E A O Y S G V L Q H L J E C S E H C I N P
L L N O Q E L A T C A P M I P D E N S E G L
A B O O P O I V M W Z T K V V S Q K Z F S O
T L K S V M B I C L L E P D R V B S M A A R
N Y B E N D J M W K Y A E T H T L U Y N V E
E S R M P D D U D R V N T O N P Q Y S C A R
M Y A Z Q E Q T Y W E I D N N F U U O L D S
N L I K G J Z L Y T F E A U E B G N E E X I
O W N B Q L P F A S H E M G T C S V I T X V
R E F L I M V E P P E E E Z A E A P T M X Z
I N O I I O R F E P R T J X Q P U L N G T S
V C R S I H D O N O Q R T U C C Q O P N F T
N T E X T M A I U W E Y E L C E I P X I O Z
E N S Y I H P S V G O N R O E T P L H T H Q
T E T U N R N L U E T H E R A R D T A E L K
Z M X X A E X H I L R N S L A Q S S M L E M
K E D K O T Z V Y C D I O N T B O H P P X Y
A L R R R S F H Y E A S S Z X A N G E E I G
Y T A G Y A U X M G I T T T W D B H R D A L
A T Z W Z S E I A Z U G E P Y G Q C E Y Q S
D E I B U I C X L I N K E D E N A A D X V O
J S L F O D Y F L I G H T L E S S N P Y I K
V T C D D E C L I N E I N H A B I T I N G O
```

Feral Cat, Islands; Consequences of Introduction

Many islands host ecologically naive animal species; that is, animals that do not have **predator responses** for **dealing** with predators such as cats.[20] Feral cats introduced to such islands have had a **devastating impact** on these islands' biodiversity. They have been **implicated** in the extinction of several species and local extinctions, such as the **hutias** from the **Caribbean**, the **Guadalupe Storm Petrel** from Pacific Mexico, the Stephens Island wren; in a **statistical study**, they were a **significant cause** for the extinction of 40% of the species studied.[21] **Moors** and **Atkinson** wrote, in 1984, "No other alien predator has had such a **universally damaging effect**."[20]

Feral cats, along with rabbits, some sea birds, and **sheep**, form the entire large animal population of the remote **Kerguelen** Islands in the southern Indian Ocean. Although exotic mammals form the bulk of the diet, cat's impact on **seabirds** is very important.[22]

Feral Cat, Restoration

Because of the damage cats cause in islands and some ecosystems, many **conservationists working** in the **field** of island **restoration** have worked to **remove** feral cats. (Island restoration involves the removal of **introduced** species and **reintroducing** native species). As of 2004, 48 islands have had their feral cat populations **eradicated**, including New Zealand's **network** of **offshore** island bird reserves,[23] and Australia's Macquarie Island. **Larger projects** have also been **undertaken**, **including** their **complete removal** from Ascension Island. The cats, introduced in the 19th century, **caused** a **collapse** in

Cat Facts, puzzle 111

```
A E S Z S C N E T W O R K Y D U T S K E O I
T J S H T A K V B G G B A S K W K V N W P V
U M D K S R L H I B U N I V E R S A L L Y W
W A A Z I I H Q E M T A X F N B W I E R H O
C B M F N B Z I L V P S D D Y Z L P Q M E U
J F A E O B R L O O N L E A G C H C L S S D
F E G X I E A A D I R S I N L U W N A Y K E
G I I G T A Y R L C U H I C T U S B C U L T
T U N M A N B G Y A R D X I A E P O I X U A
C X G T V N F E C M U E A F S T S E T K C C
A Y C T R K L R D L N S M N M N E W S A P I
P R Y N E O P E C R B A O O R E E D I F B D
M J H A S V D N R S F P Z C V K F H T E S A
I O A C N E I U L T S R R B B A F L A A H R
E D C I O G S C C E E E B C K T L D T V E E
T N O F C B F U R E M P G E U R L E S J E I
E O L I N U M R A O D L R R C E T V R R P N
L I L N Y F W K V C A G B S D D C A P O Q T
P T A G I I W E G B U R D E P N E S R E C R
M A P I J E W W K E R S E A E U F T O Z B O
O R S S Y L M O L P Y Q A B R B F A J V S D
C O E F R D M E R K F J L I O O E T E Q P U
G T W X O R N J A K R L I R H K N I C U B C
H S L V O S R G M U I C N D S B G N T A Q I
C E Z T R P G U S X L N G S F V T G S Z P N
W R S O Z L F T P Y B Q G K F D W T V P I G
Y A O R X P R E D A T O R V O T S I L U P S
C M F I B A N O S N I K T A V J C K F J E Y
```

populations of nesting seabirds. The **project** to remove them from the island began in 2002, and the island was **cleared** of cats by 2004. Since then, **seven** species of seabird that had not nested on the island for 100 years have **returned**.[24]

In some cases, the removal of cats had **unintended consequences**. An example is Macquarie Island (off the coast of Tasmania), where the removal of cats caused an explosion in the number of rabbits, rats, and mice that harm native seabirds.[25][26] [27] The **removal** of the rats and rabbits was scheduled for 2007 and it could take up to seven years and cost $24 million.[28]

Feral Cat, Hybridisation With Wild Felids

Feral cats have **interbred** with wildcats to **various extents** throughout the world, the first **reported case** occurring more than 200 years ago. The **significance** of hybridisation is **disputed**. Some old books suggested that the wildcat was a **separate** species to the domestic cat but **modern** genetic analysis[29] has shown that the domestic cat is a domesticated **version** of the near eastern wildcat (*Felis sylvestra lybica*), which is itself of the same species as the European Wildcat (felis **sylvestris** sylvestris). In some locations, high levels of hybridisation has led to **difficulties** in **distinguishing** a "true" wildcat from feral domestic and domestic hybrid cats, which can **complicate conservation efforts**.[30] Some **researchers argue** that "pure" wildcats do **not exist anymore**, but this is disputed by others.[31] One study in Scotland suggests that while "true" Scottish wildcats are unlikely to exist, the current wildcat population is distinct enough from domestic cats to be **worth** protecting.[32] For a discussion of this issue see The **Encyclopedia** of Mammals, OUP, pages 656–657.[33]

Cat Facts, puzzle 112

```
Q D R V A R I O U S W E O H B Y A Q P E N F
E P P A V U P U V W E K Z E X T E N T S F O
F G R U I E C D E R B R E T N I V Q Q I E D
P E O D R D R O X U E Q U E L X S P X I Y V
Z A J M U K E S M B L U K S T R O F F E C O
K H E S D R R P I P A L G A R W U P L I A Y
D Q C T I E Y S O O L T V R K Y N I B G D U
E P T O R G M Q Q L N I Z B A F I Z A B D U
T N Z Q M M N B S I C N C A F H N Y N X S X
R U Y R K I L I Y S S Y Y A B J T Y Y G S B
O Y T A R X X S F O Y E C H T T E U M P Q N
P J M C T Z E A P I S L P N S E N M O H C O
E L Y I C T R E D D C C V A E N D O R T W G
R A Q B P M H U G F A A Q E R I E J E K E C
Y Q O Y C N G U V S S I N H S A D M D N W Z
P L I L Q B F V E E W M H C Z T T T G C A D
M S S R E H C R A E S E R L E M R E P D L I
Z G C O N S E Q U E N C E S W T P A E D G F
L C M R L D P Q R L L R L R S D E T H D E F
T D H P N C L A V O M E R I A M U V O U L I
A A Q J M O D E R N F E X H Z P K D P H L C
Q V R R X O W N O T M E H S S J L M E N E U
Y B H Q G N I H S I U G N I T S I D V T W L
S I R T S E V L Y S S H D X D L D W X T W T
E Z T E X D N E V E S R E T U R N E D H G I
C O N S E R V A T I O N F C L E A R E D M E
S G H W C L X R Q T Z X F R V H L Q Y K C S
N P E R N I N J J H T R O W U S P N M P L P
```

Feral Cat, Zoonotic Risk

There is **concern** about the role of feral cat colonies, wild dog, and other native mammals, as a **vector** of **diseases, particularly toxoplasmosis, giardiasis** (esp. from **beavers**), rabies (e.g. **raccoons**), *Campylobacter*, **Parvovirus** and other diseases and **parasites** that can **infect** both humans and animals. Felids such as **cougars** and cats, the mammals they **feed** on, and **undercooked** meat and **chicken** are a source of *Toxoplasma gondii*, which **causes** toxoplasmosis.[34]

Feral Cat, Colonies

A feral cat **colony** (or "**clowder**") is a population of feral cats. The term is used primarily when a **noticeable population** of feral cats **live together** in a **specific location** and use a **common food source**. The term is not typically **applied** to **solitary** cats **passing** through an area. A clowder can range from 3–25 cats.[7] Their locations vary, some **hiding** in **alleyways** or in **large parks**.

Members consist of adult females, their young, and some adult males. **Unneutered** males in a clowder fight each other for **territory** and for **females**. Some will be **driven out** to find another place to live.

Feral cats who have been **trapped** in many warm areas where **fleas exist** are usually found to have a large number of fleas, causing them to be **anemic**. Both the fleas, and the food source, if **limited** to **garbage** and rodents, cause the cats to have **intestinal microorganisms** (such as **coccidia** or **giardia**) and other parasites (commonly known as **roundworms**, **tapeworms**, and **hookworms**), which lead to **diarrhea** and **subsequent**

Cat Facts, puzzle 113

```
D V B F J O A G T U O S E T I S A R A P F C
E I R B B N L I Q I P O P U L A T I O N T A
K Z T P M A N Z R N I N T E S T I N A L F M
O K I M E I P G I F I D I A R R H E A S Y P
O Q P D M D C A N E C O N S I S T G M I Z Y
C R V Y B R H R F C X H O O K W O R M S Z L
R T C N E A I B O T G I V Z G D O O I Z Y O
E R O W R I C A O O J P S J I W D I F V L B
D A L X S G K G D G R C D T E B Y H U A R A
N P O Q O B E E M E N G O P A S S I N G A C
U P N E L P N W A P O S A U W T H D N I L T
Q E Y K O P L S Y A M T R N G G C I E A U E
A D Y T C C A A P T M Z E Q I A H N U R C R
B I R F A O L N S E O S Z R U S R G T D I R
P S H T T C L O L M C G A S R C M S E I T O
A E A E I C E T W I O I E L M I C S R A R U
R A D U O I Y I W D M S F T P R T H E S A N
V S N Z N D W C H M E I I I H O W O D I P D
O E O E H I A E T G I R T S C E X N R S S W
V S C L M A Y A W C O N C E R N R O K Y L O
I A S T I I S B P A R K S X D I K J T H V R
R G O A O T C L R P K S U B S E Q U E N T M
U I U Z E R A E B L L V P R A C C O O N S S
S C R B Z L A R G E I I E W H V V B F F O N
X I C E X B F G Y R T V E E L A F D L L F W
F C E X H I K E N O A F E D R I V E N N B T
C S D N B J Z A D E E F E M A L E S J N J I
Y O M T C J Z V B R D E N Z P K L V C S G U
```

Solutions in back of book

dehydration. They also can have **ear mites**, ringworm, and **upper respiratory infections**. Others are **wounded** in mating-**fights** and **die** from the **infected** wounds. Still others eventually contract feline immunodeficiency virus or feline leukemia due to the constant transmission of blood and bodily fluids via fighting and sexual activity.

While all of these **illnesses** are quite treatable, human intervention is necessary to stop these illnesses from becoming fatal.

Feral Cat, Control and Management

In Trap-Neuter-Return (TNR), **volunteers** trap feral cats, **sterilize** them through spaying or neutering, and then **release** them, though some keep kittens or cats which are more tame. **Variations** of the program include **testing** and **inoculation** against rabies and other viruses and sometimes long-lasting flea **treatments**.[35] TNR programs are only now being introduced in some **urban** and **suburban** areas, such as Adelaide. More **recently**, such programs have been introduced in Sydney by the "**World League** for **Protection** of Animals". While various long-term studies have shown TNR is **effective** in **stopping** the breeding of cats in the wild and reducing the population over time,[36][37][38] **opponents** of TNR **frequently cite** a study by **Castillo** (2003)[39] as **evidence** TNR does not work.[40] Many humane societies and animal **rescue groups** of varying sizes throughout the United States have some type of TNR program. [41][42][43] The practice is **endorsed** by the Humane Society of the United States and the **National** Animal **Control Association**.[44] [45] While the United States **Department** of **Defense** does not **formally advocate** TNR, it does provide **information** to **military**

Cat Facts, puzzle 114

```
N D O R E P P U C Q D Y U D Y J Y O U I C Y
Y I N E E N R P U A S S O C I A T I O N R C
Z D B A O S Z O L Y E P P M O E N L L F A P
E C G J A D C M T T E S T I N G S X R O O E
E V E W N Q I U I E L O R T N O C L E R H S
A C X Z F F O M E V C C B J X G W O S M J N
R I N F E C T E D S A T F G Q G L D P A I E
E M F E H P G W T N T R I I O O E F I T E F
C Y H Y D H V E P R E F I O G M B Y R I Y E
E B G H X I R G E Q D U U A N H R R A O K D
N M T Y P I V A U E E V P O T A T M T N K W
T Y P B L B T E P C O T B F T I E S O I Z Q
L A S I X M N A Z L N Y I I Z B O K R L J Y
Y H Z B E T R G U H H L L C V F B N Y L I J
A E W N L T N N G L A I F R K Z M C S N D G
Y F T Y M I T R E N M N A T I O N A L E U E
J S O E P E N A B R U Y O L M O K I D S G N
P Q N P E D F E O S X X F P X C N N U S R D
Z T O R U B R F T M U C D F P F U P P E Q O
V T S I M L H F E A O B J O E O J Q E S X R
S C A S T I L L O C C A U C W G N U J I Y S
K Q T Z B L T E Y R T O T R F O B E E J S E
O S B A D T W W A G M I V S B M R L N G I D
R R E L E A S E R G O A V D S A K L G T Z E
G L Q R O P R O W N U G L E A D N Q D O S N
S V T B J D U O S H T E C L N U L J S U I H
E Y I D A P W N O I T A R D Y H E D A Q D D
Y M M V S P N H V N O I T A L U C O N I Y Q
```

Solutions in back of book

installations on how to **implement** TNR programs.[46] The main message from the department is that population control programs must be humane.[47]

Eradication methods include **shooting**, **trapping**, **poison baiting** and **biological** controls. For example on Marion Island cats were **infected** with the feline **panleukopenia** virus, which **drastically reduced** their population within six years.[48] The **remaining** cats were killed by shooting, trapping and poisoning. [49]

Feral cats can also be controlled by larger native predators like **coyotes**, **dingoes**, or **foxes** because many cats are too small to **defend** themselves against larger predators.[citation needed]

The **multiple**, **managed**, feral colonies at the **Colosseum** in **Rome exceed** 250 cats. Other **notable** colonies include the Canadian **Parliamentary** Cats, and the cats of **Jerusalem**.[50]

Feral Cat, Ascension Island

Ascension island was the third largest island, and one of two islands with a human population, on which feral cats had been successfully eradicated. This took two years to accomplish. Cat eradication took 14 years on Marion Island and the 25 years on Macquarie Island.[49]

The programme on Ascension island made use of live-trapping and poisoned bait – **raw fish chunks injected** with 2 mg of **sodium monofluoroacetate**, a poison which has no effect on the island's only large native animal, the **land crab**. Live trapping **replaced** poison within 1 **kilometre** (0.62 mi) of settlements to **avoid** taking domestic cats – the island's population of 168 domestic cats had been previously **microchipped**, neutered and given **reflective** cat **collars**. Domestic cats **caught** in the **traps**

Cat Facts, puzzle 115

```
H L A J G U Z I Y M K D I D V T D E WT I J
N B WJ X R O WS O E C L S G WR Y H H H L
L T T X Y E M E F R X T B O X D O L Q G I U
Z O Y H G F WY U S U R S G D P U B H C P B
F T O S I L R E F R S R T D B Y A C R S T X
M I M P L E M E N T U Y V E K O T P D E S M
S U L P I C A U G H T F T G WK E N T X F U
D O C M N T G D B B J E R U S A L E M O T E
P J I M O I D R R T B B A I T I N G E F E Q
R P X K U V U A P F V J P I L H T L Z D Z W
U A I M U E S S O L O C P O I S O N M S M I
S N I N F E C T E D H D I N G O E S A O P N
Y L N E I L H I R J R R N U G B L A N D M B
R E S L S T U C E B I O G C N Q P S A I WG
I U T J H V N A I A R I A D I T I C G U P J
O K A C C V K L Q D E Q Z I T C T E E M A S
C O L L A R S L X R D E K O O M L N D O R M
R P L D K R N Y Q X U L WV O L U S R X L W
A E A B I O L O G I C A L A H I M I R V I P
B N T N L O N Z G C E X N M S L WO E N A L
Q I I C O Y O T E S D R A WQ Q U N M O M R
D A O D M O N O F L U O R O A C E T A T E G
U I N J E C T E D F WM J WV H Z I I A N U
M B S E T R A P S S D E C A L P E R N B T Q
L M I C R O C H I P P E D E F E N D I L A L
N C L Y E X C E E D K D N V M WQ D N E R D
F G F U M O Z Y WN C Z T U E N R B G S Y P
N Y U S R Q L WV I P Z K Y H Z K U D J S F
```

were **returned** to their **owners**; land crabs and birds were released; feral cats and rats were **euthanized**.[49]

The programme was in three **phases**. A "knock–down" phase (Feb 2002 – Oct 2002) killed the majority of feral cats. During the "mop–up" phase (Oct 2002 – Jan 2004) **individual survivors** were tracked down and captured using traps, as some of these **showed avoidance** of poison bait. Finally, a "**confirmation** phase (Jan 2004 – Jan 2006) was a **monitoring** programme intended to **confirm** there were no survivors. The programme was **entirely successful** in eradicating feral cats – around 488 cats were poisoned, 73 trapped, two were shot and four captured by **hand**. However, around 38% of the island's domestic cats **disappeared** during the programme, **indicating** they had **wandered** beyond the 1 km **buffer zone** and had taken poisoned bait.[49]

Cat Facts, puzzle 116

```
P R N Z L E K K Y L E R I T N E B Q Q H X U
H O X T V K I V Q K I U D Y L T F H I I O J
A W P S S M D E Z I N A H T U E T E L U E Q
S E C R S M R B T X T R Y M R L D H K W W H
E U Z P D Z M U S Z N R E O J X V C A C V E
S V Z Y W A Q M B Q Q B G E V H L R O H X W
K L B N H X E C N A D I O V A U R K U Y T B
E S T U I Y Q T N O H N X P F I E N F G Y K
T W A S R E N W O N D H Y S U C T Q M H A Y
C W B W W X Z G F T Y I S P O B U X Y H S T
Y M L P F C J L C G N E Z N S M R A S T R T
K C F B B U M O D D C G F U B H N G H I O K
B Q X M M R N R I C L I R O I Q E W O Z U N
X V Q S E F J C U S R V T O N B D C W E D G
E E Z F I V A S T M I M R I D D J B E B P L
L U F R R T Q U A V B R A X I C S K D C O A
C U M L I J L T O J Z F I S V L X D A Q O O
B K Z N F V I R I G S B A K I E N O Z I F B
C Y G W T O S H X Y E P R T D M V A D H T L
B I B U N W L T G F P X F O U J F I C A X R
J D Z D Z X K J P E K I J J A V O T C P J X
X S A U C D W G A S D N E T L J S S K D I O
Q A L V N Q T R P G N I R O T I N O M P W H
G V P A Z Q E U F V V Y F B H Q Q Z Y I Z P
I G H M Y D M F C Z J D K O D V X D F L T M
D I C U V O J R R K B N F N K I W Q L Y T Q
M Z V Q G K D X J E A L D O X S L S J K C I
P N Q F C T H V O P I F D E R E D N A W Z R
```

Solutions in back of book

Cat Communication

Cat communication is the **range** of **methods** by which cats **communicate** with other cats, humans, and other animals. Communication methods include **postures**, **movement** (including "quick, fine" movements not generally perceived by human beings), **noises** and **chemical signals**.[1]

The communication methods used by cats have been affected by the **domestication** process.[2]

Cat Communication, Auditory Communication Methods

Cats **vocalize** with **chirrups**, **purrs**, **growls**, **hisses**, and **meows**. Meows are one of the most widely known cat sounds. In nature, the meow is a sound used by a cat to signal a request to its mother. Adult cats do not usually meow to each other, and so the meowing to human beings that domesticated cats exhibit is likely partly an **extension** of the use by kittens of this **plaintive** meow signal.[3]

The word "**meow**" (or "**miaow**") is **onomatopoeic**. Different **languages** have **correspondingly** different words for the "meow" sound, including *miau* (**Belarusian**, **Hungarian**, **Dutch**, **Finnish**, **Lithuanian**, **German**, **Polish**, **Russian**, **Portuguese**, **Romanian**, **Malay** and **Spanish**), *niau* (**Ukrainian**), *niaou* (νιάου,[4] **Greek**), *miaou* (**French**), *nya* (ニャ, **Japanese**), *miao* (喵, **Mandarin Chinese**, **Italian**), *miav/miao* or *mjav/mjau* (**Danish** and **Norwegian**), *mjá* (**Icelandic**), *ya-ong* (야옹, **Korean**) and *meo-meo* (**Vietnamese**).[5] In some languages (such as Chinese 貓, *māo*), the **vocalization** became the name

Cat Facts, puzzle 117

```
D K C H E M I C A L A N G U A G E S P J T F
S M O Y P X E N A I N A M O R U N L F R F C
A Z M R P V T O E U K I A N Y U T J Z U X G
C D M A E M O E W F I N N I S H S C Q Y J G
R O U E L A O C N S J B R U H D O S D R A Y
I M N F O A N N A S R B E R Y M X V I Y P L
D E I F Z W Y Z K L I P R V M E T O P A A G
P S C E S H S G L T I O I U I V M C D L N N
L T A J V L D U R H M Z N R X T D A N Z E I
I I T S P A N I S H C I A P F L N L L L S D
T C I C E L A N D I C N O T U N X I A W E N
H A O R W O A I M A B R E W I R O Z A R U O
U T N K Q S A R T H T G L R G O R E U L M P
A I U D B B P E W U O G G Z F H N S L L P S
N O I S E S D U G E X V I E T N A M E S E E
I N C H I T Z U R A N G E N P U X O R A G R
A B F I J S E U K R A I N I A N E V B G F R
N N H G E S B U T Z I Z O F D S E X Y I D R
A A I C E O D E K L O H N M E T H O D S K O
I I S T T R P O L I S H C N A L G J N E W C
G R S L A U M O L A T S I Z M N N E E V G O
E A E B A L D A T G R H L O O O D R P F Z D
W G S G A N I A N A C U V W X R G A T U P Q
R N Z T Y I G A N S M E S P O S T U R E S N
O U T B A C V I N I M O B I K R D S N I R T
N H J L A J F F S E S L N Z A F G B W Q N H
S J B T N Y G S N O A H E O K N L S S Z A G
K P Q Q Z F T T K K H I K E O D G D T L E O
```

Solutions in back of book

of the animal itself.

Dr **Susanne** Schötz of **Lund University** in **Sweden** provides an **acoustic analysis** of a number of felid vocalizations, including **chatters**, miaows, **murmurs**, and **combinations** of these sounds.[6]

Most cats growl or hiss when **angered** or feeling **threatened**, which serves as a **warning** to the **offending party**. If the warning is not **heeded**, a more **serious attack** may follow. Some may **engage** in **behavior**[clarification needed] or **batting** with their paws, with claws either **extended** or **retracted**. Cats sometimes make chirping or chattering noises when **observing** prey.

A "**caterwaul**" is the cry of a cat in **estrus** (or "in heat").[3][7]

Cat Communication, Purring

A purr is a sound made by most species of felines. A **tonal buzzing** can characterize differently between cats. Purring is often understood as **signifying happiness**;[8] however, cats sometimes purr when they are ill, or during **tense**, **traumatic**, or **painful** moments.[8]The purring is done to bring others to it, whether it is happy or needs **assistance**, and that is why it sometimes purrs at **unexpected** times.[citation needed]

The **mechanism** by which cats purr is **elusive**. This is partly because the cat has no unique **anatomical feature** that is clearly responsible for the sound.[9]

One **hypothesis**, backed by **electromyographic studies**, is that cats produce the purring noise by using the vocal folds and/or the muscles of the **larynx** to **alternately dilate** and **constrict** the **glottis** rapidly, causing air **vibrations** during **inhalation** and

Cat Facts, puzzle 118

```
B M S I N A H C E M P C Z N L G U Y W O U Z
L O U N E X P E C T E D V E N G S N B Q G B
S U Q R T E K D C O E I N Y N F T U I J H L
Q Y A A M M L X O J M Y F G H V Z W U E A A
R Z Y W W U T U N W S B C D K Z B E U P V C
X R O Z R G R W S R A D I N I A D R B O W I
S U O I R E S S T I P X R N D E D E E H O M
E A N A P T T T R V V R G G A N G E R E D O
I S T I H X W A I L V E C H A T T E R S O T
D S T T V K T Z C Q I M H A P P I N E S S A
U I D R A E Q E T A C O U S T I C O O K B N
T S L P U C R Y N I N H A L A T I O N D E A
S T A A R S K S T S W J F F J D W X L S Y Z
U A R R T Z B A I R E X T E N D E D S E G I
S N Y T T E M B A T T I N G P U M N O P X M
A C N Y M U I Z S H Y K L T S F O Z F X L H
N E X H A L T E R N A T E L Y R B L F E U M
N B U R E Y A H Y P O T H E S I S N E W R X
E M T H R E A T E N E D D J D A E D N A Q J
J W A R N I N G L O T T I S A Y R Y D M H B
S I G N I F Y I N G J W C L O R V O I T N T
W N S E A S E I J E V I B R A T I O N S B U
E G X G T L P A I N F U L I N H N X G G X Y
D S S U Y U Y U T F W Y M J E N G A G E X V
E O S D K N T S D U D Y A L R V L A N O T C
N R T L M D X M I J R E T R A C T E D S C Q
U C B D O N E T P S B E H A V I O R O H D M
E L E C T R O M Y O G R A P H I C S N R T T
```

exhalation.[10] **Combined** with the **steady** inhalation and exhalation of air as the cat **breathes**, a purring noise is **produced** with **strong harmonics**.[11] Purring is sometimes **accompanied** by other sounds, though this **varies** from cat to cat; in the **audio samples** that **accompany** this **article**, the first cat is only purring, while the vocal production of the second cat contains low level **outbursts** sometimes characterized as "**lurps**" or "**yowps**".

Domestic cats purr at a **frequency** of 25 to 150 **vibrations** per second.[12] **Eklund**, **Peters** and **Duthie**, comparing purring in a **cheetah** (*Acinonyx jubatus*) and a domestic cat (*Felis catus*), found that the cheetah purred with an **average** frequency of 20.87 Hz (**egressive phases**) and 18.32 Hz (**ingressive** phases), while the much smaller domestic cat purred with an average frequency of 21.98 Hz (egressive phases) and 23.24 Hz (ingressive phases).[13] Schötz and Eklund **studied** purring in four domestic cats and found that the **fundamental** frequency varied between 20.94 and 27.21 Hz for egressive phases and between 23.0 and 26.09 Hz for ingressive phases. They also observed **considerable variation** between the four cats as **regards relative** amplitude, **duration** and frequency between egressive and ingressive phases, but that this variation generally occurred within the same **general** range. A follow-up **study** of purring in four adult cheetahs found that egressive phases were longer than ingressive phases in four cheetahs. Likewise, ingressive phases had a lower frequency than egressive phases in all four cheetahs. Mean frequency were between 19.3 Hz and 20.5 Hz in ingressive phases, and between 21.9 Hz and 23.4 Hz in egressive phases. Moreover, the **amplitude** was **louder** in the egressive phases in four cheetahs.[14]

It was once **believed** that only the cats of the genus *Felis* could

Cat Facts, puzzle 119

```
C O N S I D E R A B L E O M C F U O E D S B
K R I E A E M Y N Y F Q B L D F L U R P S F
D H J A K Z T U H D Q S E H T A E R B R S U
U Y M L C Y H O H N S L O Z T H A J R O R N
L R U S P W O Y G C C H P N W X K O A D Y K
S N S T U D Y Q L K B J E B V H S A C U B G
D Q S T R O N G Y Y U M H R L A L M D C U E
T E V M L P O I A B A A J M C D O I E E O N
F K A X G N S U A D S U J C O J U C T D Z E
S D R A G E R T N U P E O F A T D T U I Q R
W O Y Z C O U U V S X M S R K V E Y H B V A
A H B V C S F Q D R P S T A S Z R O C I M L
L O N P A D C S M A X I N T H Q D G S M E X
Q Y I O U R F I N Y C D S O H P Q Z Z B J D
Y D T I I S I I N L F R U Y I Z Q C M E V E
A O K Q W T E E E O U E N R E T J K X N K N
C S E J Q D A P S B M A P G A X A S Q L E I
C E V P X A M I T T P R A B S T R R R S E B
W L I L F B V U R M U R A D G E I A B A E M
G P S L F P O Q O A E D O H T D Z O V I U O
J M S Z G V C C Z V V K I E Y M H D N J V C
Q A E F I E C Y A J V B P E Q E K W C T X T
U S R I Q A M P L I T U D E D V G P F T N N
S D G O I D U A C B E X H A L A T I O N Y J
H D E V E I L E B E V I T A L E R W D H C A
X Y N O N I C A T F F N Y C N E U Q E R F X
I M D R J V W Y Y D A E T S N S E Z F P F O
U R E V I S S E R G N I Q Z C H E E T A H W
```

purr.[15] However, felids of the genus **Panthera** (**tigers**, **lions**, **jaguars** and **leopards**) also produce sounds similar to purring, but only when **exhaling**. The **subdivision** of the Felidae into 'purring cats' on the one hand and '**roaring** cats ' (i.e. non-purring) on the other, originally goes back to **Owen** (1834/1835) and was definitely **introduced** by **Pocock** (1916), based on a difference in **hyoid** anatomy. The 'roaring cats' (lion, *Panthera leo*; tiger, *P. tigris*; jaguar, *P. onca*; leopard, *P. pardus*) have an **incompletely ossified** hyoid, which according to this **theory**, **enables** them to roar but not to purr. On the other hand, the **snow leopard** (*Uncia uncia*), as the fifth felid species with an incompletely ossified hyoid, purrs (Hemmer, 1972). All remaining species of the family Felidae ('purring cats') have a completely ossified hyoid which enables them to purr but not to roar. However, **Weissengruber** et al. (2002) **argued** that the **ability** of a cat species to purr is not affected by the anatomy of its hyoid, i.e. whether it is fully ossified or has a **ligamentous epihyoid**, and that, based on a **technical acoustic definition** of roaring, the presence of this **vocalization** type depends on **specific characteristics** of the vocal folds and an **elongated** vocal **tract**, the latter **rendered possible** by an incompletely ossified hyoid.

Cat Communication, Body Language

Cats **communicate** a **variety** of **messages** using **body language**. **Examples** include **arching** their backs as a **signal** of **fear** or **aggression**, and **slowly blinking** to signal **relaxation**. A cat that **chooses** to lie with its **stomach** and **chest exposed conveys trust**, and **comfort** (this is also typical of **overweight** cats, as it is more comfortable for them); however, a cat may also **roll** on its side or back to be able to **defend** itself with all

Cat Facts, puzzle 120

```
P S H M N A F D F G E I R Z S P R O X B D Y
S W G E Y F N O I T A X A L E R E B K W O N
O B T P W B B Y B F H L F F A V L G R B B N
H Q R I C O M M U N I C A T E Z M U D V M Q
Y E X H A L I N G E N A G G R E S S I O N S
D X I Y R C S X X A W L A N G U A G E O P M
G P N O C H E S T I L J Q S I G N A L Y O B
I O T I H O V E R W E I G H T K M K K B S G
N S R D I O A X A Y O N G J C O N V E Y S C
V E O L N S R A C C P C V A B I L I T Y I O
R D D P G E I M T H A O A U M O X S L L B M
V W U P M S E P J A R M W J Y E D S P B L R
O E C U G U T L P R D P M E M R N Y T A E M
C I E P F B Y E K A S L R P N O A T R L N D
A S D W U D Q S B C N E I A I L G I O P D H
L S G E H I I D C T O T N L E L Q G A U N B
I E B B F V A L E E W E H D E F G E R R S E
Z N M O L I X M C R J L N E E O Z R I R P T
A G B S X S N W E I E Y L A R F P S N I E A
T R U S T I C I I S T D J A B A E A G N C C
I U V I H O O Y T T S S N A C L R N R G I C
O B K F E N M T M I L A U E G I E G D D F V
N E X I O X F A R C O E G O R U N S U O I W
P R G E R F O H C S W N S E C O A H Y E C T
E X J D Y C R B R H L V M P S A N R C B D W
E L O N G A T E D Y Y I K C O C O P S E A A
I B W Q G X H T M H L F N F L C S L T A T Y
L E V J V H Z V D M B W Z Q X D X K J G Z P
```

Solutions in back of book

four sets of **claws**. Usually other signs (like ears and **whiskers folded backwards**) give an **indication** of the cat's overall mood. **Flattened** ears mean that the cat feels **threatened**, and may attack. A cat with its ears forward and keeping still while focusing on another cat (or other attacker) is being **defensive** and in a very **alert state**. **Mouth open** and no **teeth exposed** suggests a feeling of **playfulness**.[16]

The tail is often used as a **signaling mechanism**. A tail held high (**vertically**) **suggests happiness** or **confidence**, and is often used as a **friendly greeting** toward human beings or other cats (usually close **relatives**), while a half-raised tail shows less **pleasure**, and **unhappiness** is **indicated** with a tail held low. In **addition**, a cat's tail may swing from side to side. If this **motion** is slow and "lazy", it generally indicates that the cat is in a **relaxed** state, and is thought[by whom?] to be a way for the cat to search and **monitor** the **surroundings** behind it. Cats will **twitch** the tips of their tails when **hunting** or when **irritated**, while larger twitching indicates **displeasure**. A **stalking** house-cat will typically hold its tail very low to the **ground** while in a **crouch**, and move it very **quickly** from side to side. This tail behavior is also seen when a cat has become "irritated" and is nearing the point of **biting** or **scratching**. They may also twitch their tails when **playing**.[17] When greeting their owner, cats often hold their tails straight up with a **quivering** motion that indicates **extreme happiness**.[18] A **scared** or **surprised** cat may puff up its tail, and the hair along its back may stand straight up and the cat will turn its body **sideways** to a **threat**, in order to **increase** its **apparent size**. Tailless cats, such as the Manx, which possess only a small stub of a tail, move the stub around as if they possess a full tail.

Touching noses, also known as "**sniffing noses**", is a friendly

Cat Facts, puzzle 121

```
J R S Q S U R P R I S E D E T A T I R R I Y
S E T U A E N G A V B A C K W A R D S G N G
U L A I G W Z Y T M O T I O N K E S V B D N
S A L V R G B I W L I P Q O S Y L G I J I I
S T K E E Y E S S X N X E O M L A N N E C H
E I I R E L L S B A C P B N P L X I L V A C
N V N I T R F E T R R L S A L A E D Q I T U
L E G N I O R N Z S E Z A T E C D N W S E O
U S I G N A L I N G A L O W A I X U Y N D T
F P M X G N Z P M J S E O J S T R O L E G T
Y B T Z C N P P E O E O Q S U R E R K F Z E
A U N M R O T A C H N G N T R E X R C E S E
L G E E O L P H H J Q I P Q E V P U I D H T
P J R X U U R S A T F T T K I D O S U D T H
L B A T C E T R N F X U T O E R S K Q M W N
A P P R H C C H I K Z P C R R V E F N W I H
Y S P E U U I N S F U U A E V F D O M G T R
I Y A M Z A G D M D T C R J R H I L G T C H
N A L E W T R Y D H S U R I T T O D Q E H S
G W W H I S K E R S S N E N A H C E O F U E
R E Y I G A N E S A M N K C K L R D E O N T
O D J R E E A D E O D B I T I N G E M U T S
U I N U T T K L T L N D U Q N S Z B A R I O
N S G T E J P R Y O N L L C Z E E J F T N G
D H A N G S E A S I S C R A T C H I N G G A
Z L E J I L Q E G M S S E N I P P A H N U Z
F D V D A K S U R V L C O N F I D E N C E M
O V N K I N N O I T I D D A F K O H F E J E
```

greeting for cats, while a lowered head is a sign of **submission**. Some cats will **rub** their faces along their **guardian's cheek**, **hands**, or **ankles** as a **friendly** greeting or sign of **affection**. This **action** is also sometimes a way of "marking their **territory**," **leaving** a **scent** from the scent **glands** located in the cat's cheeks. More commonly, a cat will do a "head **bonk**" (or "**bunt**"), i.e., **bump** someone with the front part of its head to express affection.[19]

Cats also lick each other and people (e.g., their owners). Cats lick each other to **groom** one other and to **bond** (this **grooming** is usually done between cats who know each other very well). They will also sometimes lick people for similar reasons. These reasons include wanting to "groom" people and to show them care and affection.

Cats may paw their human **companions**, or a soft object on which they may be sitting, with a kneading motion. Cats often use this action **alongside** purring to show **contentment** and affection for their companions. This can also indicate **curiosity**. A cat may also do this when in **pain** or **dying**, as a method of **comforting** itself. It is **instinctive** to cats, and they use it when they are young to **stimulate** the mother cat's **breast** to **release milk** during **nursing**. Pawing is also a way for cats to mark their territory. The scent glands on the **underside** of their paws release small amounts of scent onto the person or object being **pawed**, marking it as "theirs," the same way they would **urinate** to mark their territory. Since the nature of the activity is an instinctive **response** related to the mother's care for the kitten, it may be an **expression** of need, **indicating** an empty **water bowl**, **hunger**, an **unappealing litter box**, or the need for some attention from the caregiver.

Cat Facts, puzzle 122

```
Y E G K T L B W M P Z R K P U F H A I I G T
Y A R G S P I J M S K A N K L E S P A C A C
L U E N Q B X Y N N T G O A Z B U M P J B E
J I E I U E I G G W P I B A T C H E E K U V
D Q T S T R S N H Y G X M A C T I O N O S I
P T I R I T I N I F U I C U Q I K N K I H T
E S N U T M G O O C Z Z B M L X Y J J G O C
B H G N O P R K U P X R G Z E A W L M J T N
E A L O N G S I D E S N K Y U J T E B N X I
D F R I Q N I B W A I E A G C S M E U B H T
I G M J V A T H F T G C R B O R C B Y W C S
S Q D E W A P F A L O S X Z M P F Q J M O N
R S A B W E E C E N R W G J F N P Q D T M I
E X B O K C I A T E X E I G O S F W X C P N
D X D X T D V E P T M S T I R W M N U A A B
N P L I N I N S U A U I S T T D T K O H N V
U D O I N T X L L B D S L X I R D X A B I D
S N P G M R U V M Q E G U K N L F N Q A O T
S B C E A F S I G R R N L I G R D Q L W N E
D N N U F R S K P Y A U A A I S S E W Y S R
E T E T R S O X J P Z P X E N G R O O M V R
T D K E I I E V P S C E N T M D P C B U E I
A N G O B O O E N A I D R A U G S I D W W T
N O N J H U A S V A L N R E G N U H J A L O
I B M W N L R A I Y B L C X Q H Y S T M K R
R E G I I Y K M B T C B R E A S T E Q B G Y
U Y A N L Q K D B D Y G N I Y D R B B M V N
G P G E S A E L E R M Y P Y U X K I B O X Y
```

Solutions in back of book

95   LowryGlobalMedia.com

Cat Communication, Biting

Although a **gentle bite** can **signify playfulness**, bites that are accompanied by hissing or growling do not **signify** playful behavior. During play, a cat can become **overexcited**, which can result in bites that, while intended only to be playful, can be strong enough to **draw blood**.

Cat bites carry a high risk of **serious infection**, **potentially fatal** in some cases. It is **important** to **wash** the **wound thoroughly** and **monitor closely** for signs of infection, **seeking medical attention immediately** if any signs of **swelling** or other **symptoms** are **detected**.[20]

When cats mate, the male tom bites the scruff of the female's neck as she **assumes** a **position conducive** to **mating**.[21]

Cat Communication, Scent

Cats can communicate through **scent via urine, feces**, and **chemicals** in skin **glands** located around the **mouth**, **tail**, and **paws**. They also use scent in order to mark their territory. **Chemically**, cat urine is made up urea, **uric acid, creatine, electrolytes, bilirubin, ketones, nitrates**, and **leukocytes**. It is the urea, however, which is highly **concentrated** in the urine of cats: the urea breaks down **intoamines** that belong to the **ammonia** group, and these **amines** further break down into **powerful**-**smelling mercaptans**. Urine spraying is also a territorial marking.[22] Cats rub up against **furniture** or **doorways** to mark the items as "theirs". When cats rub people, they are marking them with their scent, **claiming** them as "theirs".

Cat Facts, puzzle 123

```
A Q P B M S E T Y L O R T C E L E L C F Y V
E N O I T C E F N I N B I L I R U B I N L B
A C I D L I A T K E L L L U H M O U T H H A
I C W S N E N I T A E R C O E Z Y E Z L G Z
V N D E T I C X E R E V O R O X E W L U U A
Z E U C T Z T R E V C M C L S D R A W F O N
C J C E S E H R P L S A H W O J Z M P R R F
W S O F N S V K A O P C A S S U M E S E O E
I Y N A I V E I I T T P L S M R D M M W H V
A A C T N M M N A C E E H O Z I O K E O T T
M W E A G I P N L L H S N P S N F H L P F H
M R N L N S S O H U A E A T I E Q W L G U I
O O T G I C E F R W F K M T I R L C I W R Y
N O R C L E R Z C T N Y O I O A H Y N B N L
I D A W L N I I B N A R A L C R L H G O I D
A I T A E T O H K J F N Z L M A R L I I T A
T M E F W A U F J S D L T D P T L T Y N U V
T M D V S C S D K E T O N E S Y I L Z T R A
E E C H I N E G K X C U R I C S Z Z Y O E M
N D S H Y T E E P S O I E A O R Z I D A N S
T I F P E N C S I W C L Y P G N X H W M S A
I A P C T M E U O F A S F O L X O L F I U F
O T T L K E I V D C R X I M A T I N G N Y B
N E E N K S P C I N Y A N E N Y V N U E V S
D L B I T E H D A D O L G I D A I I T S E I
U Y N X Z A E R X L B C I V S F Q L B C A B
C G J G G M D C K L S P S F Y H N R U B Z L
Z A L G P N M H R H L E U K O C Y T E S O K
```

Solutions in back of book

Chartreux

The **Chartreux** is a rare breed of domestic cat from France and is **recognised** by a number of **registries** around the world. It is not recognised by the GCCF in the UK, **ostensibly** for being **too similar** to the British Shorthair, one of whose **colours** is a similar **blue-grey**. The Chartreux is large and **muscular**, with relatively short, **fine-boned limbs**, and **very fast reflexes**. They are known for their blue (grey) **water-resistant** short hair **double coats** which are often **slightly nappy** in **texture** (often showing "breaks" like a **sheepskin**) and orange- or **copper**-colored eyes. Chartreux cats are also known for their "**smile**": due to the **structure** of their **heads** and their **tapered muzzles**, they often **appear** to be **smiling**. Chartreux are **exceptional hunters** and are **highly prized** by **farmers**.

As for every French cat with a pedigree, the first letter of the official name of a Chartreux cat **encodes** the year of its birth;[1] all Chartreux born in the same year have official names beginning with the same letter. The code letters **rotate** through the **alphabet** each year, **omitting** the letters K, Q, W, X, Y, and Z. For example, a Chartreux born in 2011 would have an official name starting with the letter G.

Chartreux , History

The Chartreux is **mentioned** for the first time in 1558 by **Joachim** du **Bellay** in a poem entitled *Vers Français sur la mort d'un petit chat* (*French verse on a kitten's death*).[2] There is another representation of a Chartreux in 1747 in the **Jean-Baptiste** Perronneau's **painting** *Magdaleine Pinceloup de la*

Cat Facts, puzzle 124

```
F S I M I L A R L C H J I B E H I Z G W I G
J F C B V Y A L P H A B E T J G E Y D L O T
O A M T L W Z R B S A S I Z C D R A A J M N
S B U E W Q Y B E R R G G G E E M N D U I X
T C Z X M Y X X B K N E I S P Y O G O S T D
E H Z T A S E I O I T S I P T I T F O M T H
N A L U M L S P L S T N O X T L I M B S I D
S R E R F Q R I I R G C P P M J E E A N N E
I T S E U I M T U O C X E I K H D D V I G N
B R R O Z S P C C O A C E D Q E B D A K E O
L E J E S A T E L E X N E I R E W R I S Y I
Y U D E B U R O G E C N T E X T W M O P N T
B X A N R D U I W O O S P L W A B A P E P N
Q P A E O R X T D B O A E D U T L A A E D E
S E C U S Y E E E G T K A I N O N C X H E M
J R B L D O S N R E J D J P R R X M E S M V
Y L H R V Q I S Q X Q A Y F P T O T B Y S S
E H S O H F H L A Y T Q N J A E S X N Q U P
Z F J N Y S M I L E F B G N H R A I J P M E
I X Z B L U E G R E Y O N Q I Q M R G U V C
P H U C A I V H F H B Z I W D D C E S E E K
G I Z Z X D J T U U K N T T K T R C R J R J
H G I A F O O L W N I X N Z S Q U T S S K E
A H R R A V F Y I T W I I T L L U O L L V U
Z L J C S H N S O E K Z A C A X O R H A Z Y
J Y H N T E I L H R Y O P R V T T Y R E V K
K I H C E K G U A S C L O M Y A L L E B Q A
M R T O Q T N A T S I S E R R E T A W M G L
```

Solutions in back of book

Grange into which the cat is painted as a pet which is quite rare at this time.[3] There is a **legend** that the Chartreux are **descended** from cats brought to France by **Carthusian monks** to live in the order's **head monastery**, the **Grande Chartreuse**, located in the Chartreuse **Mountains** north of the city of **Grenoble** (Siegal 1997:27). But in 1972, the Prior of the Grande Chartreuse **denied** that the monastery's **archives held** any **records** of the monks' use of any breed of cat resembling the Chartreux (Simonnet 1990:36–37). Legend also has it that the Chartreux's **ancestors** were feral mountain cats from what is now Syria, brought back to France by returning **Crusaders** in the 13th century, many of whom entered the **Carthusian monastic order**.

The **first documented mention** of the breed was by the French **naturalist Buffon** in the 18th century. The breed was **greatly diminished** during the **first World War** and wild populations (Helgren 1997:100-103) were not seen after World War II. A **concerted effort** by European **breeders** kept the breed from extinction. The first Chartreux were brought to the U.S. in 1971 by **Helen** and **John Gamon** of **La Jolla**, **California**. In 1987, the Cat Fanciers' Association (CFA) advanced the Chartreux breed to championship status (Siegal 1997:27). There are fewer than **two dozen** active Chartreux breeders in North America as of 2007.

Historically famous Chartreux owners include the French **novelist** Colette, **Charles Baudelaire** and French **president** Charles de Gaulle.

Chartreux , Temperament

Chartreux cats **tend** to be **quiet**, **rarely making noises** such as mewing or crying, and some are **mute**. They are quite

Cat Facts, puzzle 125

```
O U Z M B J H M W O T C U A Z L V D P Y E Y
R X H W R V Y N E T R C M F O K K O F K I U
A O S A E E S E L R A H C Y T R Z W V W E O
Y A M G E Z G K U E A J M O C Y H T A P X Z
Y R K H D A H T S N G R W O Q L I N R R Q W
K X X I E F B W U A Q E E J N T Z P X O M N
H O F H R M Z J D I U B N L J A R R Z K T Z
N C I T S A N O M S D D U D Y E S S C E P J
W O R L D K C H Q U Y E F F O R T T N W I I
L N S N I I Q N X H T A D H F G V O E P S K
R C T A M N U O T T C E S N S O C D V R S P
L E R I I G I V U R I P G H E O N G O E Y L
E R A S N R E K G A T X E G R C C T W S V G
P T Q U I A T E Q C J F M D R B S X B I V Q
E E V H S N N O I S E S E O H E A E G D E S
A D Z T H D O S I D E R S G C O N J D E H Q
B S N R E E M E N T I O N N M A W O L N X R
S D G A D V A K T U E A A U H Y Q M B T K E
O D O C E B G U B B S R E D A S U R C L T C
D N W C I T K V L C A L I F O R N I A S E O
O E E S U E R T R A H C V A H Y C Y I S X R
Z T I L F M R F L A J M X K L S X L V L P D
E Q F N E O E H E L D O A W L E A J A Q A S
N K X N E H Y N E E E N L L X R D J Z U G T
O X B G O D V A T A Q K Z L U D W U E O Z I
Z A R C H I V E S E D S J T A T G E A U W U
J N O V E L I S T O D Y A L L Z Q F G B B D
A B E H D O V J M O U N T A I N S T Y P Q Z
```

observant and **intelligent**, with some Chartreux **learning** to **operate radio** on/off **buttons** and to **open screen door latches**. They take about two years to reach **adulthood**. Chartreux cats are **playful** cats well into their **adult years**; some can be **taught** to **fetch** small **objects** in the same manner as a dog. Chartreux are good with **children** and other animals. They are **non-aggressive**, **affectionate**, **good travelers** and generally **very healthy**. Chartreux tend to **bond** with one person in their **household**, **preferring** to be in their **general vicinity** (often **following** their **favoured person** from room to **room**), though they are still loving and affectionate to the **other members** of the household.

Chartreux , Popular culture

The **mascot** of the world's largest jazz festival, the **Montreal International Jazz Festival**, is a blue Chartreux **affectionately named** 'Ste Cat [1]', after the festival's hub, **Sainte Catherine Street** in Montreal.

Smokey the **Alley cat** from **Stuart Little** (1999) is of this breed.

Gris-Gris Charles De Gaulle's cat, who was following him from room to room.[*full citation needed*]

The French writer **Colette** made one of her Chartreux the **hero** of her **books** La Chatte and Les Vrilles de la vigne.

Cat Facts, puzzle 126

```
V S W G N K H A F F E C T I O N A T E L Y L
I U F W H T X I D W T R Z N B V P X T P D U
M D D E C F A V M B A M S R E L E V A R T F
P O X I O V C H I L D R E N P O M Z A E P Y
S M T O B F G E L C O L E T T E U O F F B A
B H X H B Y S R C M O P E R A T E V F E U L
O P E N E S M O N T R E A L A Q T I E R T P
O Q B C T R E S N L T O C S A M A E C R T M
K V K I N T E R N A T I O N A L L U T I O M
S U A N F H F U V Y H T L A E H O M I N N T
B U R A D I O L E A R N I N G W G W O G S K
G C E D A R L B R G N N B D L A R E N E G I
T E E R T S L I Y D H T L Y T B D W A I S G
F E T C H M O W T W F O M A F H D B T K Q Q
I E L P L O W B Q T H M A N K E Y H E X D K
O C S P N K I B J E L T A D U L T H O O D E
E R T T U E N G S E I E D E R U O V A F X R
G L U Y I Y G U S J C A T H E R I N E U O L
X I A Y L V O X T A Y T V T P P T T Z G S B
S Q R T T H A A H Z I F S W X Y E A R S S A
T R T H C I C L Z Z Q N T T S E M R M B O G
O A E I Y H N A M E D U T N C L B R S U G L
P D U B G K E I J H K P U E R L U V E O W B
J U K G M N L S C R W W J M E A S B F Z N X
E L T O H E C B V I S P O F E L E Z L I P I
D T I O Y T M L C C V O A T N H S L N V X S
P M D D E V I S S E R G G A N O N Y T Y U W
J A C Q I L I N T E L L I G E N T T X M G L
```

Cat Health

The **health** of domestic cats is a well **studied** area in **veterinary medicine**.

Topics include **infectious** and **genetic diseases**, diet and **nutrition** and non-**therapeutic surgical procedures** such as **neutering** and **declawing**.

Cat Health, Infectious Disease

An infectious disease is caused by the presence of **organisms** such as **viruses**, **bacteria**, **fungi**, or **parasites** (either **animalian** or **protozoan**). Most of these diseases can **spread** from cat to cat via **airborne pathogens** or through **direct** or **indirect contact**, while others require a **vector** such as a **tick** or **mosquito**. Certain infectious diseases are a concern from a public health standpoint because they are **zoonoses** (**transmittable** to humans).

Cat Health, Viral

Viral diseases in cats can be **serious**, **especially** in **catteries** and **kennels**. **Timely vaccination** can **reduce** the risk and **severity** of an **infection**. The most **commonly recommended** viruses to **vaccinate** cats against are:

· Feline viral **rhinotracheitis** (FVR) is an upper **respiratory** infection of cats caused by feline **herpesvirus** 1 (FHV-1).
· Feline **calicivirus** (FCV), the other common viral cause of respiratory infection in cats.

Cat Facts, puzzle 127

```
J M Q R P I Q E E L B A T T I M S N A R T E
X L V E T E R I N A R Y O P B T Z Z R O E T
M O R G A N I S M S C Z I M J Q Z O X P T A
R B R E W G A G P R E S P I R A T O R Y F N
E E B R A P I N F T B V D B P R H Y Q E C I
C D D L M J R R I S C A E I A E T Y B E T C
O I H U X N B O F M E A J R R C B R U B X C
M C T F C I O Q T R A B T P I E T P X O D A
M C E U J E R N P O H L E N D T C E V S D V
E V N N E B N S J E Z S I G O H Y T R Y W P
N W I G O P E T A P V O S A S C H P C I P C
D V C I E Z A L H I P Y A S N A Y K W N A Z
E A I G N N T R R R P L C N O L V E M F T O
D C D A N H E U E A Q E E C I I P N O E H O
I C E E A I S T R H S M X E T C I N S C O N
S I M T C E R A I Q T I C A I I I E Q T G O
E N U Q C L S E X C N T O M R V N L U I E S
A A K X V I A P T T P U M H T I D S I O N E
S T G V T Z H W Y U I R M E U R I D T U S S
E I I E U E F O I L E M O H N U R T O S X P
S O S C P E D N S N Z N N C Y S E G T O C E
T N S T K S V S P N G U L H E U C U V F P C
U E H O G M E·U K T S F Y K X D T I G Z R I
D E X R T S E R I O U S L D R P U G P S L A
I F F H U B Q M C A T T E R I E S R N O X L
E P V R T E X H N O I T C E F N I J E H T L
D X I E Z L A C I G R U S G H P N W N S X Y
C V R H I N O T R A C H E I T I S N C L N G
```

· Feline **panleukopenia** (FPV) more commonly known as feline **distemper**.

· **Rabies**, a fatal disease **transmitted** by the bite of an infected mammal. In the United States, cats make up 4.6% of reported cases of rabies infected animals.[2]

Other viruses cats may be **exposed** to include:

· **Chlamydophila** felis

· Feline **leukemia** virus (FeLV), a **retrovirus** not a **cancer**.

· Feline **immunodeficiency** virus (FIV), a **lentivirus**, and also not a cancer.

· Feline **infectious peritonitis** (FIP), a fatal, **incurable** disease caused by Feline Infectious Peritonitis Virus (FIPV), which is a **mutation** of Feline **Enteric Coronavirus** (FECV/FeCoV).

· H5N1.

Cat Health, Parasites

Veterinary **parasitology** studies both external and internal parasites in animals. External parasites, such as **fleas**, **mites**, ticks and mosquitoes can cause skin **irritation** and are often **carriers** of other diseases or of internal parasites.

Cat Health, External Parasites

· Ear mites and other mites can cause skin problems such as **mange**.

· Ticks, fleas, and mosquitoes often carry multiple **blood-borne** diseases.

Cat Facts, puzzle 128

```
L O U D E T T I M S N A R T C N L V Z D L W
W V S L O D V B V B I G W H M J L P J F K G
F W Z E O H Y U N O I T A T U M O B J P H Z
O H T M I S S L U A N R I P G P N A S O N Z
I Z K V C B H M A N G E Z N B L D N R R I U
R D H N L M A M S L N E M I O I V D T E J O
Y E E S M V Z R K E E G C Z L T J U F N C E
C C P J T V S Z N N L M R L I N I G M R I A
Z Q N M R G R C B T B Y C U W Z D R C O L I
C I H E E W L Q R I A D G E F E F X E B D N
P R N N I T V C W V R P C A G D Y B F P E E
A R N I I C S J D I U K T O B F A E H X D P
R I W M X A I I G R C H C I R E T N E S E O
A T T P M L A F D U N D G M E D D G R W Z K
S A H B V Q A I E S I B P X J A C A E H J U
I T E L G E D R M D S T O M L F A P C G H E
T I R O R B J I W I O Y S I B I R Z N G Z L
O O N O A G T Z M U T N H T N O R R A V X N
L N Z D A E J H P A U P U F H U I A C X P A
O G A X S I A U L Z O U E M N M E T J V L P
G H L I Y M D W I D D C Y O M C R P H M G T
Y Z E U A E Z Z Y L T F K F X I S X K O R K
V O V C S M P M P I R U K G L Q Y C J U H D
E Q A O F Y A Z O H D L E U K E M I A Z T Q
R L P G W L B U B R N A W I O F A T V N A F
M X C N H N S F N T X H H R O F L S Q W L X
E H X C W U E L G D H R E T R O V I R U S I
J B J H U Y C B S C O R O N A V I R U S J I
```

Cat Health, Internal Parasites

- **Heartworm**
- **Roundworm**
- **Toxoplasmosis**
- **Cytauxzoonosis**

Cat Health, Genetic Disease

- Familial **renal** disease is **inherited** in Abyssinians and Persians
- Feline **hypertrophic cardiomyopathy**
- Heart **valve dysplasia**
- **Heterochromia**
- **Luxating patella**
- **Portosystemic shunt**. Found in Persians and Himalayans.
- Flat-**chested** kitten **syndrome**

Cat Health, Skin Disorder

Cat **skin disorders** are among the most common health problems in cats. Skin disorders in cats have many **causes**, and many of the common skin disorders that **afflict** people have a **counterpart** in cats. The **condition** of a cat's skin and **coat** can also be an **important indicator** of its general health. Skin disorders of cats vary from **acute**, self-**limiting problems** to **chronic** or long-lasting problems requiring life-time **treatment**.

- Cheyletiella is a mild **dermatitis** caused by **mites** of the genus *Cheyletiella*. It is also known as **walking dandruff** due to skin **scales** being carried by the mites. *Cheyletiella* live on the skin surface of dogs, cats, **rabbits**, and humans.
- Feline **acne**

Cat Facts, puzzle 129

```
D A N D R U F F D Z T T R Y Q L O B T Y V L
E V L A V O U T A X S P R O X N K D J K S R
R A B B I T S E O P Z Q R E U G V G R J R U
M B X K I S C Y T A U X Z O O N O S I S H Z
A F F L I C T O X S T F I Z B S D W U I M R
T E U L U B X P A L J T T O L L A W K D T Y
I W H C H E Y L E T I E L L A J E Y O O D J
T R E N A L I M I T I N G U V L Q M R R Y Z
I W A L K I N G D L U X A T I N G Z S T M S
S J R V O Z C C H Y P E R T R O P H I C I A
Y Y T T P O R T O S Y S T E M I C I H A T E
N J W F R P D A I S A L P S Y D V A Q R E N
D Q O C H E L Y C N D T Z A R E I V N D S C
R D R M S Z A R I E D J W N T M G O L I I A
O O M B W M F T T D W I I U O E I B F O W W
M J G V N P S S M D W R C R L T L Z Y M N M
E Y Y I S K E H V E G A H A I X Z L J Y V S
G I K V T H O U D T N C N D T S D Z A O R T
H S H C C N G N Q I O T N M K O J I Y P D G
W K K F A U G T D R S O S I R S R U N A Y U
R H G R U T D C E E C O L C V P Q Y X T O A
Z U K T S P I T T H D H R K A P K Z Z H K G
S A I S E M E N F N I C R D Z L X X E Y D E
U A E Z S H B Q P I U Q F O E Q E R Q Q O G
I D S U E S G I B F P P J E N R M S G S C X
D K X O C O U N T E R P A R T I S B A P V O
C K R S I S O M S A L P O X O T C E G Y C S
J Z L X G D I M P O R T A N T Q L X G Q I H
```

- Feline **eosinophilic granuloma**
- Flea **allergy dermatitis**
- **Hyperthyroidism**
- **Miliary** dermatitis (feline **eczema**)
- Mange

Cat Health, Tumors and Cancer

- **Bladder** cancer
- **Bone** cancer
- **Intestinal** cancer
- **Liver** cancer
- **Lymphoma** in animals
- **Mammary** tumor
- **Mast cell** tumor
- Nose cancer
- Skin cancer
- Soft **tissue** sarcoma
- **Stomach** cancer

Cat Health, Other Diseases

- **Cerebellar hypoplasia** is a disorder found in cats and dogs in which the **cerebellum** is not completely **mature** at **birth**. Cerebellar hypoplasia causes **jerky movements**, **tremors** and **generally uncoordinated motion**. The animal often falls down and has trouble walking. Tremors **increase** when the animal is **excited** and **subside** when at ease.
- A **corneal ulcer** is an **inflammatory** condition of the cornea involving loss of its outer layer. It is very common in dogs and is sometimes seen in cats.

Cat Facts, puzzle 130

```
Q I R V W J G W O U H Y P O P L A S I A G L
K I M H H T Q O A N Y X H X R K T Q Y R L J
B K E M K Z F F P C P G D K D F Y D Z I N D
U N J V P U X C M O E Q K J S P E Z X P E F
U N Y A N I E A A O R R R D T R V G F W T F
Y D W Z U N S L T R T C E G P O P P M D T Z
O S B I A T T L W D H I F B L A D D E R N M
W M Z I K E O E P I Y N O C E X C I T E D K
Y I G H Z S M R W N R F Y N L L Y S C O E S
K S Q G J T A G T A O L R I G F L V A S R D
Z E M I E I C Y A T I A V H W X Y A P I M B
A E R I R N H E G E D M A T U R E W R N A B
G L P N K A E E L D I M K F Y R D C Q O T D
G T K X Y L B R N L S A O U J S L D U P I W
F H N T L R Y V A Z M T S V P U I E H H T C
S X T J D C B M G L G O I H E X X O E I I J
S S O G L C A I P T L R F S X M Y U E L S Q
U W R K F H B E N H O Y A D S A E K Y I V V
B L I V E R S G Y I O P P N K U R N U C J E
S H C M W Q N E X O T M C Y U A E J T O T Q
I T O E C Z E M A Z V B A Y R L V B L S R Z
D N R T R E M O R S D T D K T R O Z Y B M W
E I N C R E A S E N F H B O N E C M A P E N
Y C E R E B E L L U M I L I A R Y J A C J N
E M A M M A R Y Q P Q Y L X R M O X F D V A
G Y L A M U I N I T P P X D U T Q B L P N X
X W I I J X N T U D V B P R Q D H K H S X N
Q A D E P W L C D T D W P Z X I N I U A A S
```

· **Diabetes**

· **Epilepsy** is **characterized** by **recurrent unprovoked seizures**. Epilepsy in cats is rare likely because there is no hereditary **component** to epilepsy in cats.

• Feline **asthma**

• Flat-chested kitten syndrome

· Feline **hepatic lipidosis** also known as Feline **Fatty Liver** Syndrome, is one of the most common forms of liver disease of cats.[3] The disease begins when the cat **stops eating** from a loss of **appetite**, forcing the liver to **convert** body fat into **usable energy**.

· Feline **lower urinary tract** disease is a term that is used to cover many problems of the feline urinary tract, including **stones** and **cystitis**. The term feline **urologic** syndrome is an older term which is still sometimes used for this condition. It is a common disease in adult cats, though it can **strike** in **young** cats too. It may present as any of a **variety** of urinary tract problems, and can lead to a **complete blockage** of the urinary system, which if left untreated is fatal.

• Feline **odontoclastic resorptive lesion**

• Feline **spongiform encephalopathy**

• **Polyneuropathy**

• **Pyometra**

· **Uterine unicornis** a condition in which the female cat is **missing** a uterine horn. A **rare discovery** by **veterinarians**, the condition can be **detected** by x-ray or **ultrasound prior** to spaying if the **patient** has a **family history** of the **medical condition**. There is no known **scientific study** to **prove** that uterine unicornis is a **hereditary** genetic disorder. In some cases, the patient may also be missing a **kidney** on the same side as its missing uterine horn. This **phenomenon** is also called

Cat Facts, puzzle 131

```
W S O Y Z Y E Z X C X Z D C O M P L E T E Y
W B J G Q U R O L O G I C O M P O N E N T M
G L H X Z W W R K A E Y I Q F I H X J S B C
I P N Q S J L O D O N T O C L A S T I C S U
E N C E P H A L O P A T H Y N G I S H I P P
A A U T R T E V E L U A K O C R T U I E O C
T S T R I K E R A S R F W O O Q I L Z N N I
I K T T O C L C E A I E G K N F T T W T G V
N Y E H R Y I R C D P O C A V L S R Q I I Y
G F D X M D V T L O I P N U E Z Y A F F F V
W Z I U E A E H A V N T E H R H C S I I O U
B F M M T R R B P P L D A T T R L O N C R N
L K K H I S T O R Y E Q I R I F E U I D M P
D P Q Z Z B M C S K O H Y T Y T J N C C J R
D X E R V P R J K T U M X U I R E D T K J O
V D P H E N O M E N O N E B L O C K A G E V
W I I U T E R I N E I X I T D O N I B N P O
M S L D E T C E T E D R R C R V W D N S U K
T C E A R E S O R P T I V E O A X N I D A E
T O P L I P I D O S I S A L Z R Y E G G R D
J V S O N R Y U R H I P G B E I N Y P R H K
V E Y W A O T H D E Q P A N E E L I U T E S
I R O E R V Z R A R E X E T C T O H S D D T
J Y U R I E Y R A N I R U F I Y E K A W J A
S F N F A M I L Y C G F M G F E T S B N R K
W A G M N R X K O Y T R A G V K N C L O O M
O K Y Y S E R U Z I E S T O P S M T E E G S
B H N A X C P O L Y N E U R O P A T H Y N H
```

· **unilateral** renal **agenesis**.

Cat Health, Zoonosis

Researchers at the **University** of **Cornell** Feline Health **Center** believe that "most zoonotic diseases pose **minimal threat**" to humans. However some humans are **particularly** at risk. These are people "with **immature** or **weakened** immune systems" (**infants**, the **elderly**, people **undergoing** cancer **therapy**, and **individuals** with **acquired immunodeficiency** syndrome).

Some common and **preventable** forms of zoonosis [4] are as follows:

- **Toxoplasmosis**
- **Giardia**
- Cat-**scratch** disease
- Rabies
- Ringworm

Cat Health, Preventative Medicine, Vaccinations

Vaccinations are an important **preventative** animal health **measure**. The specific vaccinations **recommended** for cats **varies depending** on **geographic location**, **environment**, **travel history**, and the activities the animal **frequently engages** in. In the United States, **regardless** of any of these factors, it is usually highly recommended that cats be vaccinated against *rabies*, *feline herpesvirus 1* (FHV-1), *feline calicivirus* (FCV), and *feline panleukopenia virus* (FPV). The **decision** on whether to vaccinate against other diseases should be made between an owner and a veterinarian, taking into account factors **specific** to

Cat Facts, puzzle 132

```
W U U O G F P A R T I C U L A R L Y Z P T D
R Q V H A T P R E V E N T A B L E B A N Q U
L G C H G U Z D E N A C Q U I R E D Y Z Y N
U S P J F F N S F V A R M A R G O D Z C M V
L G V V M Y T I S R E V I N U R N W W B D X
M I N I M A L S L F U N D E R G O I N G N Y
I N F A N T S O N A R Q T E S C R A T C H C
A D T J I Q E M C E T E C A C C V R P H K N
G I A R D I A S G V H E Q U T I A Z F X I E
E V U R K J T A H T P V R U R I S H I D V I
N I T G H P R L E M Q J F A E X V I O H K C
E D A U T D E P E N D I N G L N A E O Y X I
S U Y F L Z C O U V A C C I N A T I O N S F
I A V E I I O X V I M M A T U R E L T D C E
S L S N Z N M O D T H E R A P Y S Z Y Y J D
O S P G B W M T R S A U S C X Y G K Z J B O
I W E A R M E A S U R E O N J L K G G U D N
L Z C G G D N D X W X R R T L U X X J N M U
A D I E E O D S T I N J Z H P G J S E N I M
E G F S N W E A K E N E D F T A X Y F C W M
F D I Y O T D J L J T S H V B E U B K W G I
C A C T I F E L O C A T I O N M M N Q E W C
N D J W S X U R E S E A R C H E R S F X J J
B K E L D E R L Y C C M H A I C O C I V E F
T F U B Z J Y R O T S I H K V L Q C Q P O D
K M P F R T L E N V I R O N M E N T Q O W F
M E J C I H P A R G O E G V D S L X P N G M
Y O N P N E X I X P S K D N J Q P I R X E F
```

the cat.

Cat Health, Preventative Medicine, Detection of Diseases

Feline diseases such as FeLV, FIV, and feline heartworm can be **detected** during a **routine visit** to a veterinarian. A variety of **tests** exist that can detect feline **illnesses**, and with early detection most diseases can be **managed** effectively.

Cat Health, Preventative Medicine, Parasite Medication

Once-a-**month topical products** or **ingestible pills** are the most commonly used products to **kill** and prevent **future** parasite infestations.

Cat Health, Preventative Medicine, Diet and Nutrition

Veterinarians commonly recommend **commercial** cat foods that are **formulated** to address the **specific nutritional requirements** of cats although an **increasing number** of owners are **opting** for **home-prepared cooked** or **raw** diets.

Although cats are obligate carnivores, **vegetarian** and **vegan** cat food are preferred by owners **uncomfortable** with **feeding** animal products to their pets. The U.S. Food and Drug **Administration** Center for Veterinary Medicine has come out **against** vegetarian cat and dog food for health reasons. Cats require **high levels** of **Taurine** in their diet. Taurine is an **organic acid** found in animal **tissues**. It is a major **constituent** of **bile** and can be found in the large **intestine**. Taurine has many **biological roles** such as **conjugation** of bile acids,

Cat Facts, puzzle 133

```
U L G F Y P U N D H O M E S Q A J J A U I F
Y T O M N F R O U T I N E H F K O S H F N N
T X I T Y D P O R T C G P O D R M J C S C P
Y Y B I L E I K D G R O H M E R P G U C R N
O P I S I T I V Z U A I N G E S T I B L E B
X B O S V E F E T N C N T J T V J A Z X A H
A L L U Y C F G C C Z T I I U W A F R S S S
Y B O E T T X A O O J A S C O G Y F E O I Y
D O G S D E F N O M M U P M U N A W Q F N C
I J I K B D D U K F S R E Z A T A T U K G G
H M C L A Y B M E O T I C S D W Q L I D Y C
G O A G L E L B D R O N I V T S X V R O T A
I N L N O N H E E T P E F A D S E I E D N K
J T O D A B E R K A I K I E L G J S M T D X
G H E X G G D S T B C X C L E E O I E Z D G
S S D H A N E K S L A V I T Z D P T N N K P
P Z E X I I R D A E L P A E L J I D T M E C
U Q T O N T A T R M S R K S O L K N S Q Q I
R C A Y S P P L R H I I D T Z V I Q G C Q Z
T F L C T O E I F A L C N S X O T K O K L G
L V U E I C R Y N T N E U T I T S N O C M Y
G M M T V D P O R A C O M M E R C I A L M Y
W M R G U E A L L O K G S E O S C L F O R B
V L O A G R L H V E E F H Q W Q T W T K D W
A Q F Y W B E S E R S A K G Q N I I W S S J
P F D N O I T A R T S I N I M D A G N H V A
O X G M E C K E J O M K H W I V Y D B E Y E
X T D U C U X M V B T T U H N I U G F M Y L
```

antioxidation, **membrane stabilization** and **modulation** of **calcium signaling**. It is essential for **cardiovascular function** in cats, and development and function of **skeletal** muscle, the retina and the **central nervous** system. Although meat protein can be **substituted** with **vegetable proteins**, vegetable proteins don't require **sufficient** amino acids which are vital for a cats body to function.[5][6]

Cats can be **selective eaters**. Although it is extremely **rare** for a cat to **deliberately starve** itself to the point of **injury**, in **obese** cats, the sudden loss of weight can cause a fatal condition called Feline Hepatic Lipidosis, a liver dysfunction which causes pathological loss of appetite and **reinforces** the starvation, which can lead to death within as little as 48 hours.

Pica is a condition in which animals chew or eat **unusual things** such as fabric, plastic or wool. In cats, this is **mostly harmless** as they do not **digest** most of it, but can be fatal or **require surgical removal** if a large amount of **foreign material** is **ingested** (for example, an **entire sock**). It tends to occur more often in **Burmese**, **Oriental**, **Siamese** and **breeds** with these in their **ancestry**.

Cat Health, Food Allergy

Food allergy is a non-**seasonal** disease with skin and/or **gastrointestinal** disorders. The main **complaint** is **pruritus**, which is usually **resistant** to **treatment** by **steroidal** anti-inflammatory drugs. The exact **prevalence** of **food allergy** in cats remains unknown. There is no breed, sex or age **predilection**, although some breeds are commonly affected. Before the onset of **clinical signs**, the animals have been fed

Cat Facts, puzzle 134

```
X A N T I O X I D A T I O N D H I S T I R G
L V E G E T A B L E Y L T S O M V U X M B A
J S U B S T I T U T E D S S E L M R A H I T
E F U N C T I O N R H M E R I U Q E R A Y R
E L J R D D E L I B E R A T E L Y C C N G E
F C A B T S S U R G I C A L Y Q K L W C R A
R S N S M C D F A O P R O T E I N S T E E T
A Z I E U B E P O S L L A V O M E R Z S L M
L C J G L F B N U O N W E S E M A I S T L E
U Z R F N A F O T G D X S G N I H T E R A N
C N E E K A V I I R E N T I R E N Y E Y N T
S O S A S R L E C T A I N G E S T E D O G L
A I I M E E R I R I T L E C G M K H I R R O
V T S N C O M U N P E L V M Q Q I T M Y L R
O C T H F B D R H G A N G U S D A U B K L L
I E A E F T W B U N D A T G N Z H M A A E A
D L N Y D D E B O B X K N C I U A N T M Z C
R I T E X X R S H Q A Z S L A T S N G I S I
A D N O I T A L U D O M I T E L E U V G A N
C E U N A E R P I C A B R R E I C S A U G I
E R E N S F X J M G A Y I Z R R E I E L N L
A P S U C C I V X T T A P O G L O A U G D C
T Q E K O B T I S J L S Q C E H D I N M U W
E S B C Q T S E G I D R S C D N X Y D P W L
R I O O L L A N I T S E T N I O R T S A G U
S C Y S E V R A T S L I M E M B R A N E L V
A Q Y R U J N I L S V S E C R O F N I E R R
S B R E E D S Y G E Y X C L A T E L E K S Y
```

Solutions in back of book
```
```

the **offending** food **components** for at least two years, although some animals are less than a year old. In 20 to 30% of the cases, cats have **concurrent** allergic diseases (**atopy** / flea-allergic **dermatitis**). A reliable diagnosis can only be made with dietary **elimination-challenge** trials. **Provocation** testing is necessary for the **identification** of the **causative** food component(s). **Therapy** consists of **avoiding** the offending food component(s).[7] Cats with food allergies **constantly itch** their red, **hairless**, and **scabby** skin. Hair loss usually occurs on the face and/or anus. The most **popular prescription** diets for cats with food allergies include **Hills Science Diet** d/d or z/d.[citation needed] It may take, depending on the severity of the **reaction**, two weeks to three months for a cat to **recover** if the offending allergen is **removed**. **Immediate results** may not be seen.

Cat Health, Malnutrition microminerals

Malnutrition has been seen in cats fed **homemade** or vegetarian/vegan diets[citation needed] produced by owners with good **intentions**[citation needed], and most **published recipes** have been only **crudely balanced** (by **computer**) using **nutrient averages**. [citation needed] Because the **palatability, digestibility**, and **safety** of these recipes have not been **adequately** or **scientifically tested**, it is difficult to **characterize** all of these homemade diets. [citation needed] Generally, most **formulations** contain **excessive protein** and **phosphorus** and are **deficient** in **calcium, vitamin** E, and **microminerals** such as **copper, zinc**, and **potassium**. [citation needed] Also, the **energy density** of these diets may be **unbalanced** relative to the other nutrients. Commonly used meat and **carbohydrate ingredients** contain more phosphorus than calcium. Homemade feline diets that are not actually deficient in

Cat Facts, puzzle 135

```
M A Y D I E T H E R A P Y G Q W C N O J M M
I M S I F O R M U L A T I O N S N I L I M I
B J A G R E C I P E S T M N M H O X H D P C
F H H E N E R G Y L D B M U U C O P P E R R
D S D S X W V L A S A F E T Y D K C O N O O
E C E T C I U O I C N L D R P C T O E T T M
C M H I O A P S C I P C I I R O V N M I E I
N W S B M F B I N E M R A E O N P C M F I N
A R I I P K D B N N R B T N V S O U A I N E
L G L L O D I D Y T Y V E T O T T R L C V R
A Z B I N G R E D I E N T S C A A R N A P A
B G U T E P D V U F O N J G A N S E U T R L
N E P Y N S G O Z I J F T I T T S N T I E S
U Z S R T H E M C C P V F I I L I T R O S G
C I C G S I V E R A H B F E O Y U Z I N C E
A R A E C L S R U L O A G A N N M K T W R L
R E U V I L S N D L S L L A T D S Q I Z I I
B T S I E S D C E Y P A R L N O I H O H P M
O C A T N R C Q L D H N E F E T P N N A T I
H A T A C S A J Y P O C S X I N E Y G I I N
Y R I M E P L G E V R E U L C T G S N R O A
D A V I W Q C A E C U D L G I E C E T L N T
R H E N N N I I M S S J T X F U S H O E A I
A C A D E Q U A T E L Y S A E H G S Y S D O
T T W F J U M N D Q A V O I D I N G I S Z N
E S C O M P U T E R E A C T I O N X E V Z N
U H O M E M A D E R M A T I T I S X I W E J
N O S Y O A P A L A T A B I L I T Y U C B S
```

Solutions in back of book

fat or energy usually contain a **vegetable oil** that cats do not find **palatable**; therefore, less food is eaten causing a calorie deficiency.[citation needed] Rarely are homemade diets balanced for **microminerals** or **vitamins**.[citation needed] Owner **neglect** is also a **frequent contributing factor** in malnutrition.[8]

Cats fed **exclusively** on raw, **freshwater** fish can develop a **thiamine deficiency**. Those fed exclusively on **liver** may **develop vitamin** A **toxicity**.

Cat Health, Obesity

Neutering and **overfeeding** have **contributed** to **increased obesity** in domestic cats, especially in **developed countries**. Obesity in cats has **similar effects** as in humans, and will **increase** the **risk** of **heart disease**, etc. thereby **shortening** the cat's **lifespan**.

Cat Health, Toxic Substance

The ASPCA lists some **common sources** of toxins[9] that pets **encounter**, including: **plants**,[10] human **medications** and **cosmetics**,[11] **cleaning products**,[12] and even foods.[13]

Some **houseplants** are harmful to cats. For example, the **leaves** of the **Easter Lily** can cause **permanent** and life-**threatening** kidney **damage** to cats, and **Philodendron** are also **poisonous** to cats. The Cat Fanciers' Association has a full list of plants harmful to cats.[14]

Paracetamol or **acetaminophen** (trade name **Panadol** and **Tylenol**) is **extremely toxic** to cats, and should not be given to them under any **circumstances**. Cats lack the necessary

Cat Facts, puzzle 136

```
Y D N D T K Z A C I R C U M S T A N C E S C
Q H Z D U G J P P H I L O D E N D R O N I V
P R Q K V R D F E D E P O L E V E D N O M Y
P Z L W L U F Z P E Q C P R O D U C T S I L
A B I J Q H V R M F I O B E S I T Y R E L J
C O M M O N K Z I I I N W X R U H H I C A L
E M F X R T J P D C C T P T G M I I B R R C
T O X I C H O W H I O R E R L I A H U U E Y
A C J J F E Y Q K E U I O E A Q M N T O M L
M X J X A C Q Q F N N B A M F N I P E S X E
I N C R E A S E D C T U C E I K N N D N U V
N P A L T A B L E Y R T D L M N E J P K T I
O D Z Z H L E H N G I I S Y E Q E A K F U S
P W S P R Q M H C B E N V N D A R R K W F U
H O U S E P L A N T S G E W I A N K A V R L
E E I D A M A G E T T O G V C M P I O L E C
N Q K L T O X I C I T Y E E A K A V N S S X
F J J I E A S T E R V N T P T I N T D G H E
A O U L N K B X B S T A A O I S A R I C W S
C H M Y I Z I J N J M E B I O T D M S V A C
T Y L E N O L R T O H W L S N C O F E L T I
O T I A G C I P L G S J E O S E L F A K E T
R H V J G S H O R T E N I N G F G N S T R E
V U E Z K P E E J N V D O O Z F Y L E E P M
T D R D I Q A V B V A I G U Z E Y R E W I S
V E O J R F R E Q U E N T S E Y E B G C H O
E N C O U N T E R S L I F E S P A N H C T C
Y H P F B R I G N I D E E F R E V O E T B Y
```

glucuronyl transferase enzymes to safely break paracetamol down and **minute portions** of a **normal tablet** for humans may prove fatal.[15] Initial symptoms include **vomiting**, **salivation** and **discolouration** of the **tongue** and **gums**. After around two days, liver damage is evident, typically giving rise to **jaundice**. Unlike an overdose in humans, it is rarely liver damage that is the cause of death, instead **methaemoglobin formation** and the production of **Heinz bodies** in red blood cells **inhibit oxygen transport** by the blood, causing **asphyxiation**. **Effective treatment** is occasionally possible for small doses, but must be **extremely rapid**.

Even **aspirin**, which is sometimes used to treat **arthritis** in cats, is much more toxic to them than to humans and must be **administered cautiously**.[16] Similarly, **application** of **minoxidil** (**Rogaine**) to the skin of cats, either **accidental** or by well-meaning owners **attempting** to **counter** loss of fur, has sometimes **proved** fatal.[17][18]

In **addition** to such **obvious dangers** as **insecticides** and **weed killers**, other common household **substances** that should be used with **caution** in areas where cats may be **exposed** to them include **mothballs** and other **naphthalene** products,[16] as well as **phenol** based products often used for **cleaning** and **disinfecting** near cats' feeding areas or **litter boxes**, such as **Pine Sol**, **Dettol** (**Lysol**), hexachlorophene, *etc.*[16] which, although they are widely used without **problem**, have been sometimes seen to be fatal.[19] Ethylene glycol, often used as an **automotive antifreeze**, is **particularly appealing** to cats, and as little as a **teaspoonful** can be fatal.[20] **Essential oils** are toxic to cats and there have been reported cases of serious illnesses caused by **tea tree oil**, and tea tree oil-based **flea treatments** and **shampoos**.[21][22][23]

Cat Facts, puzzle 137

```
N O I T A V I L A S F A N T I F R E E Z E A
J O C K S A T T E M P T I N G I Q W S B X I
Q G N I T C E F N I S I D D R T U I P P P N
D A N G E R S U B S T A N C E S Q Q R O O S
S P A Y C A U T I O U S L Y K I L L E R S E
Y P A L O W D T R E A T M E N T S D B T E C
O E C R U I D M A O M I N O X I D I L I D T
D A C A N A L E I S P M W R S R C E A O O I
M L I L T U G T T N P S Z G B H A U D N I C
I I D U E T L H E T I H N M O T U P D S E I
Z N E C R O C A L O O S Y A G R T H I I V D
E G N I D M X E B N X L T X R A I E T D O E
L I T T Z O Z M A G Y O R E I T O N I I M S
L J A R C T Q O T U G S A X R A N O O K I A
I A L A S I F G E E E Y N T O E T L N H T P
T U I P G V D L A A N L S R G C D I F T I P
T N G T R E E O E P Z T F E A L X N O E N L
E D A M N G E B X A B B E M I E K H R N G I
R I S P E E W I O G F D R E N A O I M Z L C
I C P O H L S N N X M V A L E N B B A Y U A
F E I I O T B S K L E S S Y P I V I T M C T
O V R L N P H O E N F S E V N N I T I E U I
K C I S W E M A R V G O H I Z G O H O S R O
M I N U T E S A L P R O V E D K U F N Y O N
I B C E N O G O H E I N Z N G O S M V Y N L
S M O T H B A L L S N O R M A L B P S Y Y N
E V I T C E F F E O T E A S P O O N F U L J
O D O M M J R D I S C O L O U R A T I O N T
```

Tabby Cat

A **tabby** is any domestic cat that has a coat **featuring distinctive stripes**, **dots**, **lines** or **swirling patterns**, usually together with a mark **resembling** an M on its **forehead**. **Tabbies** are sometimes **erroneously assumed** to be a cat breed.[1] In fact, the tabby **pattern** is found in many breeds, as well as among the general mixed-breed population. The tabby pattern is a **naturally occurring feature** that may be **related** to the **coloration** of the domestic cat's **direct ancestor**, the **African Wildcat**, which (along with the **European** Wildcat and **Asiatic** Wildcat) has a similar coloration.

Tabby Cat, Tabby Patterns

There are four tabby patterns that have been shown to be genetically distinct:[1][2] **Mackerel**, **Classic**, **spotted**, and **ticked**.

A fifth includes tabby as part of another basic color pattern. The "**patched**" tabby is a calico or tortoiseshell cat with tabby patches (the latter is sometimes called a "**torbie**").[1]

All those patterns have been **observed** in random-bred populations. Several additional patterns are found in specific breeds. A modified Classic tabby is found in the **Sokoke** breed. Some are due to the **interaction** of **wild** and **domestic** genes. **Rosetted** and **marbled** patterns are found in the Bengal breed.

Tabby Cat, Mackerel Tabby

The Mackerel tabby pattern has **vertical**, **gently curving** stripes on the side of the body. The stripes are **narrow** and may be

Cat Facts, puzzle 138

```
W L F G Z R A A I T S X D A X A R N C N M T
M T L W A K Q M D N Z D Q B J K U L O F U J
W W I L D C A T P U L G E N T L Y B C K G R
F O R E H E A D I H N S W M T M E Z G L X W
E R O S E T T E D I N T E R A C T I O N F E
A R W E W G T A R M K N D C S F K T V J U R
T A S T Q I J R B W O O M P P E R L G A Y E
U N M W U K U T U W F O O L N A K I A Z N H
R K A A I C K R E L A T E D K T T T C K R V
E J D T C R H J C X T M L S D U O C J A O N
J U C O U K L X M E G H P L T R N R H P N Y
K G O C M R E I D H P D I O Y I F G B E C E
I U Z M U E A R N Z G W A U B N R Q G I D L
P L Q B O R S L E G N V B N G G U R Z P E L
M A N I L G V T L L I D E V R E S B O V U D
D O T S F X Z I I Y L M F B B O P H I E R V
G E W T T I I K N C B G Z X R O W T F R O E
G R L A E R S Y K G M J G I K J C I J T P S
M R I B S R I O E Y E B L N D N O C Z I E S
L O N Z R S N P K C S P J L I X L K E C A F
L N E V D A U S E X E I K T Q F O E W A N G
E E S Y R S M M R S R E S P V M R D S L C I
Q O O C J I O V E K O I D B B K A C I E E E
E U K R T A D V O D D I R E C T T U X F S S
L S O G T T A B B I E S T G D N I V I H T U
S L K J S I I L T Y B B A T G Z O U F C O S
E Y E E X C I S S A L C N Y X O N S K R R G
A R W T P E H F B P H G F H T V E A F Z I G
```

continuous or **broken** into bars and spots on the **flanks** and **stomach**. An "M" shape appears on the forehead along with **dark lines** across the cat's **cheeks** to the **corners** of its eyes. Mackerels are also called '**Fishbone** tabbies' probably because they are named after the mackerel **fish**.[3] Mackerel is the most common tabby pattern.

Tabby Cat, Classic Tabby

The Classic (also known as "**Blotched**" or "Marbled") tabby tends to have a pattern of **dark browns**, **ochres** and **black** but also occurs in **grey**. Classic tabbies have the "M" pattern on their foreheads but the body markings have a **whirled** or **swirled** pattern (often called a "**bullseye**") on the cat's sides. There is also a light colored "**butterfly**" pattern on the **shoulders** and three **thin stripes** (the center stripe is dark) running along its spine. The legs and tail have dark **bars** as do the cat's **cheeks**.

Tabby Cat, Ticked Tabby

The **Ticked** tabby pattern produces hairs with **distinct** bands of color on them, **breaking** up the tabby patterning into a **salt**-and-**pepper** appearance. **Residual ghost** striping or "barring" can often be seen on the lower legs, face and **belly** and sometimes at the **tail tip**.

Tabby Cat, Spotted Tabby

The **Spotted** tabby may not be a true pattern,[citation needed] but a **modifier** that breaks up the Mackerel tabby pattern so that the stripes appear as **spots**. Similarly, the stripes of the Classic

Cat Facts, puzzle 139

```
J Z S T O P S P O T T E D W J M P R P S T S
K N E L P D N I X T G V N W O U O Z Y R Q F
R J P X G M R O H N J Y W O Z R X R D E C V
Z N I P V I R A R V Y H W L B H U W T D X U
D A R K B R O W N S W P A L M H B T S L L T
J M T M K U D E G I T U J Y A C S K D U N F
K M S T O M A C H Z D Q I K M F E I V O Y V
C M F H S X B Q F I T E A U W E X L F H I E
H O Q T A I L E S X O A E X H G N P T S W A
E D R M L M T E D X Z Y P C K K E Q I S V J
E I V N T A R U B Y E H Y I Y X F Q W J F B
K F J T E K W J Y S H B W L P O X I U Q S P
S I N F A R S G L J J G C H Q B R D E N W X
G E R Y T O S L F E V O Y E I L C K K H J F
H R H T W Y U D N L N W A E E R T Z Z B U I
O A E G P B E G M T A V K D Q F L R P S P W
S R I Y K K N B I R B N H D L Q W E L V U R
T S Q O C I D N H L T B K E C Y X O D D R W
K Y E I K R U B A P H C L S B Y X P K O Q B
S D T A X O G C I E M I N O U X J I R F C S
L R E H U Q K F R G G Z D I T V M T K K P T
B R A S I T E L I V F T C D T C T Z D C P P
B R Y B I N A E L S R T H H E S H S M W S M
E O O V P B M Q I T H J Z L R J I E G Z G U
L O R K G G D S N N Y W R Q F S B D D P A Z
L W P Z E K M R E Y S E T M L L C G X U N A
Y C J B P N X Y S Z N P X P Y Z N T C H F G
S R Z O C H R E S Q P E P P E R F W C R E L
```

tabby pattern may be broken into larger spots. Both large spot and small spot patterns can be seen in the Australian **Mist**, **Bengal**, Egyptian Mau, Maine Coon, and **Ocicat** breeds.

Tabby Cat, Genetic Explanations

The tabby patterns are due to 3 distinct gene **loci** and one **modifier**:

The **agouti** gene, A/a,[4] controls whether or not the tabby pattern is **expressed**. The **dominant** A expresses the underlying tabby pattern, while the **recessive** non-agouti or "**hypermelanistic**" **allele**, a, does not. Solid-color (black or blue) cats have the aa **combination**, **hiding** the tabby pattern, although sometimes a suggestion of the underlying pattern can be seen (called "ghost striping"). However, the O gene for **orange** color **suppresses** the aa genotype, so there is no such thing as a solid orange cat.

The **primary** tabby pattern gene, Mc/mc, sets the basic pattern of stripes that underlies the coat. Mc is the wild-type tabby gene and produces what is called a 'Mackerel striped' tabby. 'Classic' tabbies are cats who also possess mc, a recessive mutant gene that produces the blotched pattern.

The Ticked tabby pattern is on a different gene **locus** than the Mackerel and Classic tabby patterns and is **epistatic** to the other patterns. A dominant mutation, Ta / ta, **masks** any other tabby pattern, producing a non-patterned, or 'Agouti' tabby, with **virtually** no stripes or bars. If the Ticked tabby pattern gene is present, any other tabby pattern is **masked**. Cats **homozygous** for the ticked allele (Ta / Ta) have less barring than cats heterozygous for the ticked allele. When a cat of this genetic make up is **selectively bred** for lack of barring and wide banding on the **hair shaft** the resulting pattern is referred to as **shaded**.

Cat Facts, puzzle 140

```
Z A V G P W B K H J E D R X X X Z X L W D D
C T L E Y S H N G W T V C Y H I G R K H Q K
Z W O N Q W W O M G E P I S T A T I C R Z W
B U S Q M I Y G S Z M L Y E S H A F T S C Y
N P L K Y N X I J N P T I Q N Y Z M C H A I
P E Q Q B O S H Q B C M V U B P Z A I B C U
W U M H B G T T C P Z U E L Y E K S J S M U
P M H W V S A G T T R X Z G D R Y K U X T S
P Q X Y B D B Z P U S G V U J M A S O F L R
N G H C T C B S A Q B S I U Y E A M J Y V M
G I G Y A X D F M O R F M A L L N S I L F T
I V T P H Z O B H K D Z M P G A S S K R J L
K R E I O A M O D I F I E R A N G A J E P Z
K C H B M E I P D G D J H S H I O O P C D W
K O N G O E N R Z B I I J G Q S N O U W D N
V U Y I Z L A L L E L E N E X T R D T T E X
G T F N Y P N C E N O L P G P I D Q S G I N
B A C Q G B T V X G C K C N U C R H P R B J
X G H X O Y I I P A I K M H M O S X E M X B
H V D J U S Q R R L T A C I C O R A N G E J
R A V D S H H T E R V V O E T G S E L E I A
P I X E L A R U S U P P R E S S E S O Y U I
Y B C Z X D X A S E L E C T I V E L Y U V O
B E L L A E A L E D C O M B I N A T I O N E
R S S B O D H L D Y H R C S R Z X T L F M Q
W O B X R X G Y R K L P Z U X E F R E X X X
E M C D G H C B M Y I J P K S N D F M M N Y
L V C F U M P M T P C T Y J O I K F I G Y P
```

Solutions in back of book

131

LowryGlobalMedia.com

Tabby Cat, Etymology

The **English** term "tabby" comes from the 1630s, "striped silk **taffeta**," from the French "**tabis**," meaning "a rich, **watered silk** (originally striped)," from Middle French *atabis* (14c.), from Arabic *attabiya*, from *Attabiy*, a neighborhood of **Baghdad** where such **cloth** was first made, named for **Prince 'Attab** of the **Omayyad dynasty**. Compare to Spanish "**ataviar**", meaning to **decorate** or to **dress** or **wear** (often **implying** very **elegant** and/or **expensive clothing**).[5] The term tabby cat, "one with a striped coat", is **attested** from the 1690s; the shortened form tabby was first attested in 1774. The idea of "female cat" (1826) may be influenced by the feminine proper name Tabby, a pet form of **Tabitha**, which was used in the late 18c. as **slang** for "**difficult old woman**."[6]

Tabby Cat, History

Since the tabby pattern is a common wild type, it might be assumed that **medieval** cats were tabbies. However, one writer believed this to be **untrue**, at least in England. Some time after the mid-17th century, the **natural philosopher John Aubrey** noted that **William Laud**, the **Archbishop** of **Canterbury** was "a great lover of Catts [*sic*]" and "was presented with some **Cyprus-**catts, i.e. our Tabby-catts". He then claimed that "I doe well remember that the common English Catt, was white with some **blewish piednesse** (ie, grey and white) : sc, a **gallipot** blew. The race or breed of them are now almost lost."[7]

Cat Facts, puzzle 141

```
N D A Y B N T X D Q G A X K B R K R C A Y N
M H J L K U N T R U E L E G A N T L M X T Z
V O S I Z X Z A T T E S T E D E P J L M V W
A V A V I A R V T A F F E T A R V S Y J Q I
K U S C S E Q Y T U K T E N L U E O C O A E
K I B L E WI S H G R S C P G V R S K H Y O
P WZ R A H T I B A T A R J E L A E S N R V
J WD M E D I E V A L I L C V C I D L O I I
H X Q R U Y X D V A N B E H L N L S Q H B H
W Q S G S W E E L C C N M L S O H M H L K O
Q B S T D R R U E C O Y I T WG T J B B WA
H K D X E X P E N S I V E O L N Z H Z Q Q R
C A N T E R B U R Y X Y M P M U J K I T K U
L R A T T A B I Y A A A U I F Z E WJ N D R
O WB L N P A A Q U I M P L Y I N G H X G J
T E WO M A N N R L T X C L WO Z P A C B Y
H A D O L V T B L C O U Q A T T A B I Y A P
Y R T T M D I I F M H I D G A D D U A L H Q
L J J A L A WT D K H B A G H D A D K Z P F
K P T M B U Y I X F N P I E D N E S S E H J
B Y Y V D I C Y P R U S E S V N N R T F A M
N X T N WI S I A X F I I J H V S M G Q D E
U WL S L A N G F D F R A L D O Z D B G G W
Q A Z O A T T A B F P F G L K D P Z C L X A
W C P B N N O P K M I Y D F P R K J U K J V
N Z A S M P Y K S P A D E C O R A T E K S Q
U Z Q L J I Y D O V E N M L K H A H U Q J G
Y I H E Z X E E R R E H P O S O L I H P T B
```

Point Coloration

Point coloration refers to animal **coat** coloration with a **pale body** and **relatively darker extremities**, i.e. the **face**, **ears**, **feet**, **tail**, and (in males) **scrotum**. It is most **recognized** as the coloration of Siamese and related breeds of cat, but can be found in rabbits, rats, sheep, and **horses** as well.

Point Coloration in Cats

Point coloration in cats is a form of **partial albinism** resulting from a mutation in **tyrosinase**, an **enzyme involved** with **melanin production**. The **mutated** enzyme is heat-**sensitive**; it **fails** to work at **normal body temperatures**, but becomes **active** in **cooler** areas of the skin.[1] As a result, **dark pigment** is limited to the **coldest** areas of the body, that is, the **extremities**. **Pointed** kittens are **born white**, since the **womb** is **uniformly warm**. As the kitten ages, the cooler areas **darken** while **warmer** areas **remain cream** to white in color. Points are not limited to solid colors or dark colors. It is possible to have a red (orange color) or fawn (pale warm gray) point. It is also possible to have a tortoiseshell or tabby point. This coloration is also sometimes called *colorpoints*.

Because of this **restriction** of pigment, pointed cat's eyes are always some **shade** of **blue**, because the top layer of the **iris** is not covered in another color, letting the blue show through. The back of the eye also lacks pigment, giving these cats' **pupils** an **eerie red reflection** in the dark, unlike a normally pigmented cat's **green** to blue **shine**.

The point gene is carried on the C **locus**, where **pure** albinism is

Cat Facts, puzzle 142

```
S I H A L K L U D G O M X F X G Z L F V R Y
G E N I V N O I T C E L F E R L X P P W E S
V N B Q J L E M T E R M P E R A T U R E S D
L L Y S C R O T U M X S V S N Y D V W D T B
W U U Z T O S A B E B U T S E D L O C M R N
Q K D D Y R O F V K O M L L N A C Z W S I J
T V F I N V O L V E D D O J Z R O O H N C E
H A L I T O A P E C Y D Y W L K L R C I T K
M M C E V I T C A R T C G U P E O S C N I A
M T B T A O C H W E W S E N L R R A L A O M
U M P P N D O H Y A H U U I M A P A I L N T
T G S D W R I J F M R Z L F E T O U M E Q Y
A M I G S P O Q P A B M B O D Y I L R M E Z
T U C E G Q P B O P I C B R S G N M R E D D
E I S E N S I T I V E L O M H W T K E Z K C
D X L X O L G X N I E M S L J V S N M N K S
A P T T R E L A T I V E L Y O W P H A E F C
R A Q R M T E F E G F M P T W R D U I S J D
K R E D E W O R D A R K E N F P A L N N V T
Z T A M E M S E I T I M E R T X E T W U E I
W I S P Y P I G M E N T J I V Q G C I W T X
E A Q W P Z A T Y R O S I N A S E C Q O D R
L L O C U S N L I D V P R O D U C T I O N G
J T G M Y S D E E E Y F C M S I N I B L A I
G R E E N O R M A L S H A D E S R O K V M O
B V I E T C L P X Y A A A C P U P I L S V B
V D R Y F M D E Z I N G O C E R B Z S V U M
L Y U X V R E M R A W H I T E T A I L H Q W
```

Solutions in back of book

also carried. It is **shown** with the sign cs, and needs two **alleles** of cs for the points to be **expressed**. Also carried on the C locus is the gene for the **sepia pattern**. This is the darkest of all of the pigment **restricting** patterns, and pigment is only **paled** at the warmest point in the body, the **abdomen**. This pattern's **gene** is **represented** by cb. When a cat carries the genes cs and cb, the **mink** pattern is **formed**, in which the pigment **distribution** is between a sepia and a point cat.

Cat Breeds with Points

- **Balinese**
- **Birman**
- **Colorpoint Shorthair**
- **Himalayan**
- **Javanese**
- **Peterbald**
- **Ragdoll**
- **Siamese**
- **Siberian (Neva Masquerade)**
- **Snowshoe**
- **Tonkinese**

Cat Facts, puzzle 143

```
U H X J T H R E S E M A I S D M Z I J S Q L
A J K C M L X O X V A G N N E H S J T T U Z
X X Z A J S H P R D E J O C S I G Y N W K M
K R U S M B H N N N L Y A O E M K A I A T T
N D R T R N K S M I F K V N N A A L O W S K
N E M O D B A V B Q G V Q K I L P L P I R V
A T B X I T Q Z M D V T V O L A X E R H R W
C N N T D U C Y M I N K R M A Y C L O D J I
I E K K Z G J P F S K Y B P B A A E L J I A
Y S R E S T R I C T I N G E V N H S O G V F
W E S W Y Q C L U R R G Z S B B V Q C Q H D
S R S H O R T H A I R H S E I Q I Q R F U F
G P N Q G J S E K B Z K R N R M C H A J W I
T E R D E M R O F U B R X A M P F A U M N P
X R E O N C W Q C T N I B V A D Z E H A H E
U E T H E U H R R I N Q V A N A A D R A Z T
B Z T K O R T C Z O W U O J E U I X Q M M E
C L A A E C Y S O N P A L E D X L S V V E R
H H P M X K M A I P E S Y U F C Y G O O O B
W O N N V R X T I H N E B G I A V E N Z H A
R A G D O L L S I B E R I A N L I U L T S L
Y N X X A M G H W L M U H T R B M H B F W D
V X Q H D T U O T G D E S S E R P X E O O E
Q R T C V Q U W O C S P Z Q S O P V Q U N Z
F Y H J B C D N C W M A S Q U E R A D E S L
U X R A O T O N K I N E S E B N Y Z Z W Y E
K H X O D H K V Z H C U Y C C F K J U L J O
U F T I D E Z F M S D J G Q D K D P M W X P
```

Solutions in back of book

Persian Cat

The **Persian** is a long-haired breed of cat **characterized** by its **round** face and **shortened muzzle**. Its name refers to **Persia**, the former name of **Iran**, where similar cats are **found**.[dubious – discuss] Recognized by the cat fancy since the late 19th **century**, it was **developed** first by the English, and then mainly by American breeders after the Second World War. In Britain, it is called the Longhair or Persian **Longhair**. The **selective** breeding **carried** out by breeders has **allowed** the **development** of a wide **variety** of coat colors, but has also led to the **creation** of **increasingly flat-faced** Persians. Favored by fanciers, this head **structure** can bring with it a number of **health problems**. As is the case with the Siamese breed, there have been efforts by some breeders to **preserve** the older type of cat, the *traditional breed*, having a more **pronounced** muzzle, which is more popular with the general public. **Hereditary polycystic kidney disease** is prevalent in the breed, **affecting** almost half the population in some countries.

The **placid** and **unpretentious nature** of the Persian **confers** a **propensity** for **apartment living**. It has been the most **popular** breed in the United States for many years but its **popularity** has seen a **decline** in Britain and France.

Persian Cat, Origin

It is not clear when longhaired cats **first appeared**, as there are no known long-haired **specimen** of the African wildcat, the ancestor of the domestic **subspecies**. There were claims[by whom?] in the 19th century that the gene responsible for long hair was

Cat Facts, puzzle 144

```
Q C Z B L Y F M Y T I S N E P O R P Y I H X
R S H P A Z X N M I V N Y T G B T Y G G N K
Q F I W C N B I F R N X Z N S W S F F P N V
K G U I M L V E P Z B N D E M S F R K O K V
I F S Y N N N R S O S L O N G H A I R J F U
H O D D E C L I N E L T I I I S F E C V D N
F C E N T U R Y O O D Y R V T X P J H D O P
P O P U L A R E Q I T K C U I A Q W A E I R
S N V I K M H V A R I E T Y C N E T R C L E
P F I R S T D T H S T D F E S T G R A A K T
E E K I D N E Y L W I K Q E K T U D C F U E
R R P J K R V W I A G N A K C K I R T T Q N
S S O O S P E C I M E N G T W E E C E A T T
I H F U Q P L A C I D H G L X O L B R L L I
A E O D N X O R F D F Y L S Y S G Z I F V O
F R U R A D P R O B L E M S U I Q H Z Q D U
F E N E T D M I D K M Q P B F K D C E U L S
E D D U U E E E E R Y A S J D Z P M D W M K
C I J X R R N D A A G P O P L A R I T Y Y L
T T O Y E A T E Y D E P O L E V E D U O M I
I A E O M E C E D C E K I O S R Y C V Q A E
N R L J Y P H D I S E A S E Y B S R Y G V Q
G Y A L X P R E S E R V E I E J V A R L R L
L X U N O A S E L E C T I V E B B W I Y G M
R V Y Z M W I Y R J C F Z E N J G Y X N E T
A P A R T M E N T S P R O N O U N C E D J W
J M E X X G F D I L F Q Y U Y J M G T X C P
S W A T G O H I A V H P H F Q B D W K O G Z
```

Solutions in back of book

introduced through **hybridization** with the **Pallas** cat, but research in the early 20th century **refutes** this theory.[citation needed]

The first documented ancestors of the Persian were imported from **Khorasan**, Persia into Italy in 1620 by **Pietro della Valle**, and from **Angora** (now **Ankara**), Turkey into France by **Nicholas-Claude Fabri** de **Peiresc** at around the same time. The Khorasan cats were grey coated while those from Angora were white. From France, they soon reached Britain.[1] Longhaired cats were also imported to Europe from Afghanistan, Burma, China and Russia. **Interbreeding** of the various types were common especially between Angoras and Persians.[2]

Recent genetic research **indicates** that **present day** Persians are **related** not to cats from the Near East but to cats from Western Europe. The researchers stated, "Even though the early Persian cat may have in fact originated from ancient Persia, the modern Persian cat has **lost** its **phylogeographical signature**."[3]

Persian Cat, Persians and Angoras

The first Persian was **presented** at the first **organized** cat show, in 1871 in the **Crystal Palace** in London, England, organized by **Harrison Weir**. As specimens **closer** to the **later** established Persian **conformation** became the more popular types, attempts were made to **differentiate** it from the Angora.[2] The first breed standard (then called a *points of excellence* list) was issued in 1889 by cat **show promoter** Weir. He stated that the Persian differed from the Angora in the tail being longer, hair more **full** and **coarse** at the end and head larger, with less pointed ears.[4] Not all cat fanciers agreed with the **distinction** of the two types, and in the 1903 book "The Book of the Cat" **Francis Simpson**

Cat Facts, puzzle 145

```
T D D O H D T F X N N Q P M T W F G C T M U
V I J W L O N L P N Q B X K W F R N C R S S
X X K U Y U E E Q F J W R X C G T C L I L J
R E P Z Z B D G F C T Q T U S Z E S C Y F F
H Y B R I D I Z A T I O N R A N P S R H R G
J B B P A L L A S B S T P G O A J L D U A U
U R R M I Y W E R K H O R A S A N A J N N S
D V K E F E L O R O A P L O K R G Q P P C Q
I N D I C A T E S I G N A T U R E Q K H I J
F I E M D N P R A E K N X L G Y E B K Y S J
F T L U X K E W O S W H A R A L Y B C L G A
E D L U D A Q O E K D F F H J C P L C O O J
R G A R V R T H C I B C H W S A E U W G E W
E P T D F A K S A P R E S E N T E D L E W F
N O I T A M R O F N O C R H A R R I S O N M
T I N D B O E C N E L L E C X E X S T G F A
I N T S R C L O S E R U S O W F H T A R Q H
A T E Q I E A T R N R C L A U D E I K A F S
T S R E F U T E S G H Z O P N F E N G P H A
E I B L U S E A L A A S A A R Z P C O H B V
D M R C L T D T L N E N A R R O I T N I A K
H P E I R E S C M B D B I L O S M I L C X J
N S E V A Y S Q F U L L J Z O H E O X A Q A
L O D A Y U S N R I Z A A D E H G N T L O H
N N I L R Z R T S D N S K T B D C V S E Y W
O U N L C Y H T A U V V O I E J F I Z I R M
X D G E R Z T P O L R Z N I N R X X N Y V A
D C G J X J V L F I T S E Q J Q X X Z B X W
```

states that "the distinctions, **apparently** with **hardly** any difference, between Angoras and Persians are of so fine a nature that I must be **pardoned** if I **ignore** the class of cat commonly called Angora".[5]

Dorothy Bevill Champion lays out the difference between the two types in the 1909 *Everybody's Cat Book*:[6]

> Our pedigree imported long-hairs of to-day are **undoubtedly** a cross of the Angora and Persian ; the **latter possesses** a rounder head than the **former**, also the coat is of quite a different **quality**. The coat of the Persian consists of a **woolly** under coat and a long, hairy outer coat. In **summer** it loses all the thick **underwool**, and only the long hair **remains**. The hair is also somewhat shorter on the shoulders and upper part of the hind legs.

> Now, the Angora has a very different coat, consisting of long, **soft** hair, **hanging** in **locks**, **inclining** to a **slight curl** or **wave** on the under parts of the body. The hair is also much longer on the shoulders and hind legs than the Persian, this being a great **improvement**; but the Angora fails to the Persian in head, the former having a more **wedge**-shaped head, **whereas** that of the modern Persian **excels** in roundness.

> Of course Angoras and Persians have been **constantly crossed**, with a **decided** improvement to each breed; but the long-haired cat of to-day is **decidedly** more Persian-bred than Angora.

Champion **lamented** the lack of distinction among various long-haired types by English fanciers, who in 1887, decided to group

Cat Facts, puzzle 146

```
S N K C Y R K N O B Q Q F P Q J Y K E Y F F
C P H C X F W U N D E R W O O L C C A G E J
X Y N Z C D E R E X U N D O U B T E D L Y A
Y P X B E E L T H Y H Y R T O N C X K B F N
D I G U C O N S T A N T L Y V L O H A T H T
L K M U V E S Q W X N M S K O N L L N Z C T
B H X H M W U D A B Q G B R S G M Y A K K T
G N Z A Y L R K K S C O I N C L I N I N G K
N N L R Y W B Q T G J W U N R B L X K U F J
Z Z G D O T P W X X Z W N M G F E I A S U K
F P M L E X C E L S A A A B R E M M U S I Z
T X M Y F C R O S S E D C T E Q C P B A X K
S T W L J B I X V S Z E I U M A Q R I E C F
A P C U R L L D E N L C H Q A A F O X J O Y
N R C E A V W S E Q T I O U I Y C V Q A D Q
S V G E W Z S V X D H D L M N S F E R J I H
S I X A B E V I L L E E L S S W P M P Q O J
G A K G S L I G H T R D R L S W K E I B L T
C F E S O F T G M J Z L E C A H G N K E L S
C H O I E B N E P Q A Y M V J E L T V G E O
H P A R D O N E D T D S E S Q R D A A D B T
G T S M M O J Q U A L I T Y S E R U Z E L K
K O F A P E R L Z A A A G M U A E H G W F E
R P Y B Q I R O L V O W T N R S Z B E B U O
R S R U X O O A T T G M W T O W A F M U I M
U K S T H M E N P H B N L Z E R U C M R S W
K B S H S K C O L C Y A P P A R E N T L Y X
E U L Z Y F C U V Q I G K N G K X F G E K V
```

them under the **umbrella term** "Long-haired Cats".[6][2]

Persian Cat, Traditional Persian

The Traditional Persian also known as **Doll Face** Persian is considered to be essentially the original breed of Persian cat, without the development of **extreme** features. The CFA however **regulates** the peke-face, flat-nose "**ultra**" Persian as the "**true**" **standard** for this breed. The **recently-named Traditional** breed has not change its physical appearance but some breeders in America, Germany and Italy and other parts of the world started to **interpret** the standard **differently**, and thus developed the ultra over time, as the result of two genetic mutations.

Persian Cat, Peke-face and Ultra-typing

In the late 1950s a **spontaneous** mutation in red and red tabby Persians gave rise to the "**peke-faced**" Persian, named after the flat-faced **Pekingese** dog. It was registered as a breed by the CFA but fell out of favor by the mid 1990s due to serious health issues. In fact, only 98 were registered between 1958 and 1995. Despite this, breeders took a liking to the look and started breeding towards the peke-face look. The over-**accentuation** of the breed's characteristics by selective breeding (called *extreme-* or *ultra-typing*) produced results similar to the peke-faced Persians. The term peke-face has been used to refer to the ultra-typed Persian but it is **properly used** only to refer to red and red tabby Persians bearing the mutation. Many fanciers and CFA **judges considered** the shift in look "a **contribution** to the breed."[1][7][8][9]

In 1958, breeder and author P. M. **Soderberg wrote** in "Pedigree

Cat Facts, puzzle 147

```
M S B Q D Q H B Z U Z N T K M A D D V R F H
R F M C R P S H P X I A M R W C E Y P N Z D
R Y X N Y G I R H P O P G H D C J V L R O V
Q S E L C L X E B P F J U D G E S Z A Y A Z
I V O P W A T E E R J Q K M B N P E N J W J
Y P W C K E A N A G S K X K B T O K O E Y P
T E R M H I F C E M E R T X E U N C I G B A
L K O P A H L N M R T N M J K A T O T T N V
D I T A N S M H E X E A Y C L T A N I Y A D
Q N E P R W H Q S M L F H F P I N T D B M E
I G K N A V T V D L Z R F Z L O E R A R E C
G E Y U J L C R E C K W L I W N O I R T D A
R S T M P A A R T N E U V X D E U B T U Y F
T E I H Q D B R C D A J L F C D S U M T J E
N N S P N M S N O A F C P D I R H T C J X K
U B Y A U Z J Y C R G H N E F T W I L C L E
D D T C L V J W E A Q X X L P V U O O O T P
X S W E T T K F V D G I X V Q L O N N P C V
K D G C R C I N T E R P R E T A Q H A C E G
Y W T A A H B B V S N E G R E B R E D O S V
O V B F Y L T N E C E R G W G E T T B Z X R
O Q X N I S P W T J K Y J U Y O R E T B D U
J G Q J V M M O H O X T U M L U C P A G D U
F D C U S E D D T G E O O X E A X N M U W R
N H O M K Q G S O J O Q X S G P T X E L O L
Y I D L X C P R O P E R L Y M B P E J J B A
N X H R L K B G F Q A K O C Q L V A S O E S
A N B A R A V I V V O C O N S I D E R E D D
```

Solutions in back of book

Cats, Their Varieties, breeding and Exhibition"[9]

> **Perhaps** in **recent times** there has been a tendency to over-accentuate this type of short face, with the **result** that a few of the cats seen at shows have faces which present a peke-like appearance. This is a type of face which is **definitely recognized** in the United States, and helps to form a **special group** within the show classification for the [Persian] breed. There are certainly disadvantages when the face has become too short, for this **exaggeration** of type is **inclined** to produce a **deformity** of the **tear ducts**, and **running eyes** may be the result. A cat with running eyes will never look at its best because in time the fur on each side of the nose **becomes stained**, and thus **detracts** from the **general appearance** [...] The nose should be short, but perhaps a **plea** may be **made** here that the nose is better if it is not too short and at the same time **uptilted**. A nose of this type **creates** an **impression** of **grotesqueness** which is not really **attractive**, and there is always a **danger** of running eyes.

While the looks of the Persian changed, the Persian Breed Council's standard for the Persian had **remained basically** the same. The Persian Breed Standard is, by its nature, somewhat open-ended and **focused** on a rounded head, large, wide-spaced round eyes with the top of the nose **leather placed** no lower than the bottom of the eyes.[clarification needed] The standard calls for a short, **cobby** body with short, well-boned legs, a **broad chest**, and a **round** appearance, everything about the ideal Persian cat being "round". It was not until the late 1980s that standards were changed to limit the development of the extreme appearance.[citation needed] In 2004, the **statement** that

Cat Facts, puzzle 148

```
Y B G F J Q Z L X I K P W E R X J D X B U E
K N J D B M F T Z M I N C L I N E D G L T Y
L F U L B M X U Z Z K A T T R A C T I V E I
Y M G R O T E S Q U E N E S S E M S X G S V
D E R R A P P E A R A N C E I T I A E J Y O
O B P E O A L F N U B D F R E G F G I Q J I
R I Y P S U R E C O G N I Z E D S M T L E O
N C C L F U P H A D Y Z H E F A P Z R G H L
F Q N F E U L E A T H E R Y N R T I M E S F
S G A O S T A T E M E N T L E F T E O K X H
N R E C I S I X C W Y N I S X J Q C S K Z I
L I B U Z T N N X W T Y S R W E K O T I N X
X X N S E D A M I W S I D D E T L I T P U G
J Z T E Y F L R L F O G D C N M J W O S Y V
F Q P D J X X O E N E V Y E G E A B Y W U B
C Y E E U X X U E G F D C R F P W I E O F C
P D V D R C T N O W G E G O W O S R N R I P
D A E J O H T D A C R A W Y B L R L Z E A D
Q N Y N C H A S H Z F A X D R B C M L A D U
R G E D I Z G P G P C H B E O J Y A I J E I
M E S Z L A W S S L O X N R A G I G Z T U T
P R A F G Q T Z A A J M T B D C E F S J Y Z
Y J K T J O W S L C H E S T E N E G Y A P S
L S T C A R T E D E Y A G P E J F T P B N V
L S E M O C E B S D W P S R P Y P C U S W P
Y B A S I C A L L Y K Q A V H V B X H B I C
R J R U N N I N G C X L K Q C I Q N H W C P
R L H R A B E N V J Z Z T V G L V H B A G A
```

muzzles should not be **overly pronounced** was added to the breed standard.[10] The standards were **altered** yet **again** in 2007, this time to **reflect** the flat face, and it now states that the **forehead**, **nose**, and **chin** should be in **vertical alignment**.[11]

In the UK, the standard was changed by the Governing Council of the Cat Fancy in the 1990s to **disqualify** Persians with the "upper edge of the nose leather above the lower edge of the eye" from **Certificates** or **First Prizes** in **Kitten Open Classes**. [12][13]

While ultra-typed cats do better in the **show ring**, the public seems to prefer the **less extreme older** "doll" face" **types**.[1]

Persian Cat, Himalayan

In 1950, the Siamese was **crossed** with the Persian to **create** a breed with the body type of the Persian but **colorpoint pattern** of the Siamese. It was named **Himalayan**, after other colorpoint animals such as the Himalayan **rabbit**. In the UK the breed was recognized as the Colorpoint Longhair. The Himalayan **stood** as a separate breed in the US until 1984, when the CFA **merged** it with the Persian, to the **objection** of the breed councils of both breeds. Some Persian breeders were **unhappy** with the **introduction** of this "**hybrid**" into their "**pure**" Persian **lines**.[14] [15]

The CFA set up the registration for Himalayans in a way that breeders would be able to **discern** a Persian with Himalayan **ancestry** just by **looking** at the pedigree **registration number**. This was to make it easy for breeders who do not want Himalayan blood in their breeding lines to **avoid individuals** who, while not necessarily **exhibiting** the colorpoint pattern, may be carrying the point coloration gene **recessively**. Persians with

Cat Facts, puzzle 149

```
M N N R D S Z W X Q Q N A K T A A L A K R W
Y A I R P I N D I V I D U A L S Z R N H O C
A Q A Z L F O I G E E N J S N L U M Q Y X K
C U G V F A T V R Z J K E W D N X U W B B W
G O A Z Y U E U A R D T Y A C B Z C F X B Q
P P L E S S P C W F A L E J G F S K G M P S
L S J D N N Q F F C E H I C H I N C H A E W
M W D E E M J M I V E N A R S T D Y Y N X H
N R M P F R Q F I R T L D I S C E R N S H J
J E O E J X I S O R I R Y D M U W P L G I R
X B Z K K T S F O G E Z S D E C T W B N B H
A M P X R E A D N F D H U E I G P R B A I B
M U J E C E U M L I I U M W Z N R W Y Y T Y
D N C E U C E E R M E H Z G O E E B A I P
I J R U T N C D S S R A N G O I G V M L N O
S L K I T T E N G T N C T T N T I K E A G P
Q U O V E R L Y X C D I N D Q C S L U M J A
U N Y E I R B E E B R V I D R E T G B I C T
A H C R P F A S T Q H L O E F J R Y L H W T
L A V T C R T B T A K N P C C B A V P Y Z E
I P T I N R I S B V H J R N L O T H C E Q R
F P C C Y J O Z N I A B O U A O I P K F S N
Y Y J A F Z L S E B T S L O S M O W K G T H
F J W L S J G K S S E T O N S L N K M M S V
A H F H Y B R I D E G O C O E Z G A I Q Q Z
I O Y W Y Q T U N J D O O R S V Z P E N C Y
M Y E D O L L I N E S D M P E L F J R S G X
W E H V A C R E A T E C H T D E R E T L A I
```

Solutions in back of book

Himalayan ancestry has registration numbers starting with 3 and are commonly referred to by breeders as colorpoint carriers (CPC) or 3000-**series** cats, although not all will **actually carry** the recessive gene. The Siamese is also the **source** for the **chocolate** and **lilac** color in solid Persians.[16][17]

Persian Cat, Exotic Shorthair

The Persian was used as an **outcross secretly** by some American Shorthair (ASH) breeders in the late 1950s to "**improve**" their breed. The hybrid look **gained recognition** in the show ring but other breeders unhappy with the changes **successfully pushed** for new breed standards that would **disqualify** ASH that showed signs of hybridization.

One ASH breeder who saw the potential of the Persian/ASH cross proposed and eventually managed to get the CFA to recognize them as a new breed in 1966, under the name Exotic Shorthair. **Regular outcrossing** to the Persian has made present day Exotic Shorthair similar to the Persian in every way, **including temperament** and **conformation**, with the **exception** of the short **dense** coat. It has even **inherited** much of the Persian's health problems. The **easier** to **manage** coat has made some label the Exotic Shorthair the **lazy** person's Persian.

Because of the regular use of Persians as **outcrosses**, some Exotics may carry a copy of the recessive longhair gene. When two such cats **mate**, there is a one in four **chance** of each **offspring** being longhaired. **Ironically**, longhaired Exotics are not **considered** Persians by CFA, although The **International** Cat **Association accepts** them as Persians. Other associations register them as a **separate** Exotic Longhair breed.[18]

Cat Facts, puzzle 150

```
C O N S I D E R E D H S N P K O C N G T C B
I N C L U D I N G A I N L E F E Y O C B X S
P R D E S N E D K M P O T X Y D O I H P U R
N E O K U N T D P S M K N L H V J T O H Z K
B G A N V A H R H Q S Q L D G D O P C A K N
Y U N S X H O N I D Z A E F I V L E O B C X
U L O S I V Y Z A L C T U S L S T C L E K Z
V A I C E E M Q L I I O Q V I P N X A U V G
S R T D E N R O N R G U H B L F E E T M C L
S N I Z J D H O E B A A I W A I M R E A I P
O M N L C P R H G L J U I M C O A S U U B E
R U G L A I N R I A X G X N T A R E J D Y C
C H O R I I G F A S C Q G M E F E R S H L R
T D C G I A Y N T L O C N H T D P I C J L U
U I E G A N A M I O O O E M H X M E U I U O
O N R H B Z X D C R I U A P A F E S C N F S
J T C P P X I F Y T P G T T T T Y R N S A
E E K X R K U R A Q V S Y C C S E Z O M S C
C R Y U U Z R I I T V D F L R A U I N H E C
N N Q M S A C L Q B E R U F L O T E M J C O
A A S T C O G W I H B S B L O A S J I C C M
H T D T S V C Q S Y V S Z D M C U S T L U J
C I M S N M S U H B V I U R S A R T I J S A
T O A J C T P O U T C R O S S E S C C N R L
P N O Y F L H H U R M F M P S W Q C M A G M
L A K W K O W S Q U N O X Y Y B A G Y A M Y
E L D Y S L N U F O L L B W Y I E R A B Q C
S E C R E T L Y C Z E T A R A P E S Y D E J
```

Solutions in back of book

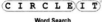
Cat Facts, puzzle 76

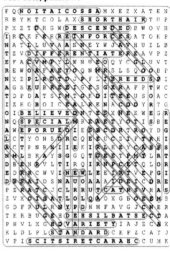

Cat Facts, puzzle 77

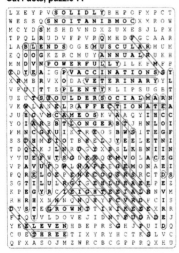

Cat Facts, puzzle 78

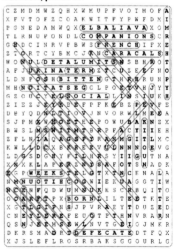

Cat Facts, puzzle 79

Cat Facts, puzzle 80

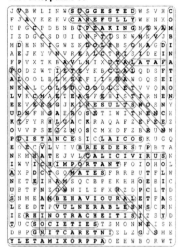

Cat Facts, puzzle 81

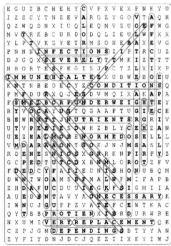

Cat Facts, puzzle 82

Cat Facts, puzzle 83

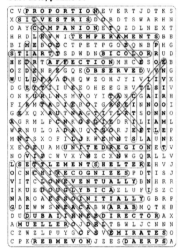

Cat Facts, puzzle 84

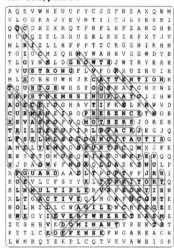

Cat Facts, puzzle 85

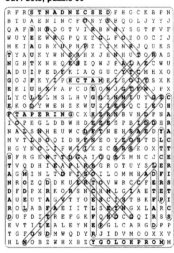

Cat Facts, puzzle 86

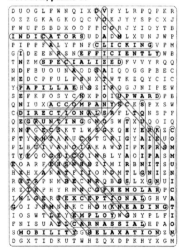

Cat Facts, puzzle 87

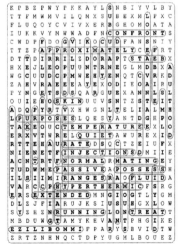

Cat Facts, puzzle 88

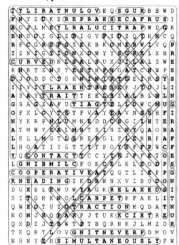

Cat Facts, puzzle 89

Cat Facts, puzzle 90

Cat Facts, puzzle 91

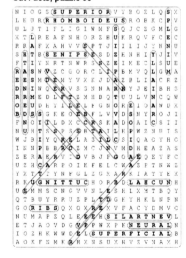

Cat Facts, puzzle 92

Cat Facts, puzzle 93

Cat Facts, puzzle 94

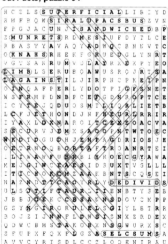

Cat Facts, puzzle 95

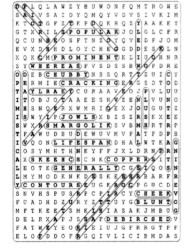

Cat Facts, puzzle 96

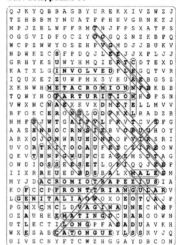

Cat Facts, puzzle 97

Cat Facts, puzzle 98

Cat Facts, puzzle 99

Cat Facts, puzzle 100

Cat Facts, puzzle 101

Cat Facts, puzzle 102

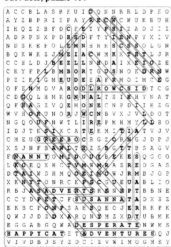

Cat Facts, puzzle 103

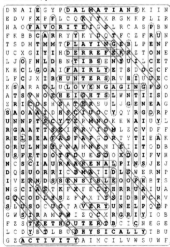

Cat Facts, puzzle 104

Cat Facts, puzzle 105

Cat Facts, puzzle 106

Cat Facts, puzzle 107

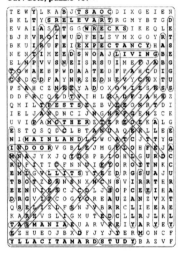

Cat Facts, puzzle 108

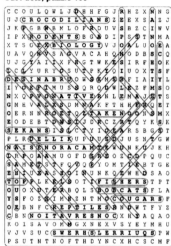

Cat Facts, puzzle 109

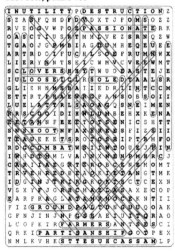

Cat Facts, puzzle 110

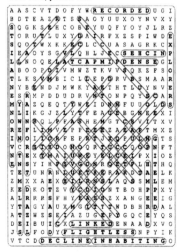

Cat Facts, puzzle 111

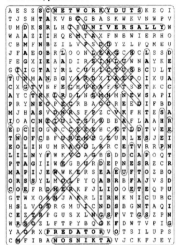

Cat Facts, puzzle 112

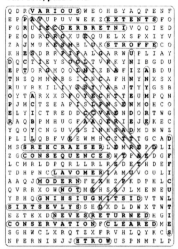

Cat Facts, puzzle 113

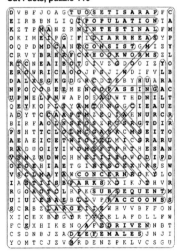

Cat Facts, puzzle 114

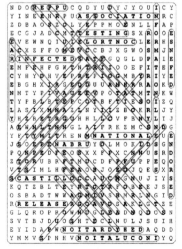

Cat Facts, puzzle 115

Cat Facts, puzzle 116

Cat Facts, puzzle 117

Cat Facts, puzzle 118

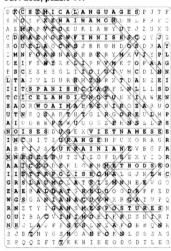

Cat Facts, puzzle 119

Cat Facts, puzzle 120

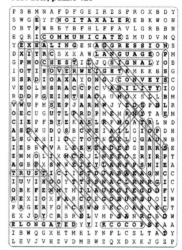

Cat Facts, puzzle 121

Cat Facts, puzzle 122

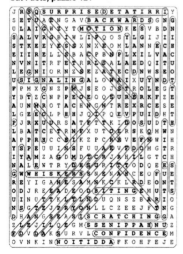

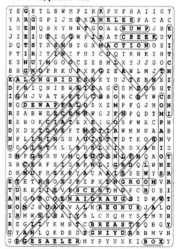

Cat Facts, puzzle 123

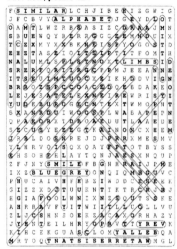

Cat Facts, puzzle 124

Cat Facts, puzzle 125

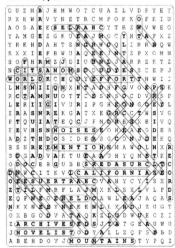

Cat Facts, puzzle 126

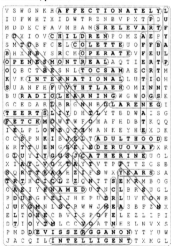

Cat Facts, puzzle 127

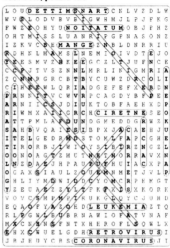

Cat Facts, puzzle 128

Cat Facts, puzzle 129

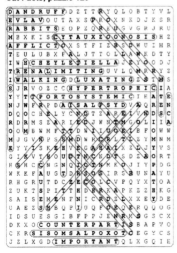

Cat Facts, puzzle 130

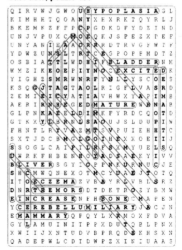

Cat Facts, puzzle 131

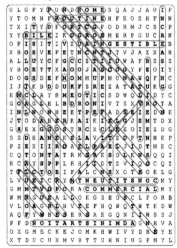

Cat Facts, puzzle 132

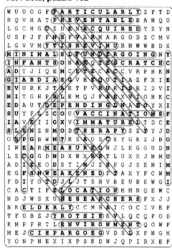

Cat Facts, puzzle 133

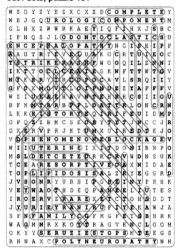

Cat Facts, puzzle 134

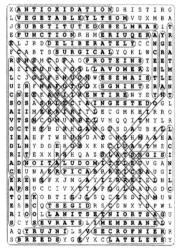

Cat Facts, puzzle 135

Cat Facts, puzzle 136

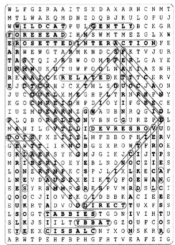

Cat Facts, puzzle 137

Cat Facts, puzzle 138

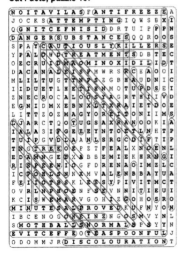

Cat Facts, puzzle 139

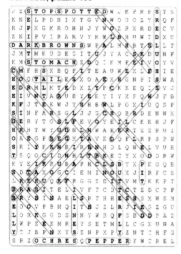

Cat Facts, puzzle 140

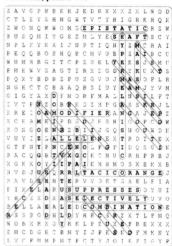

Cat Facts, puzzle 141

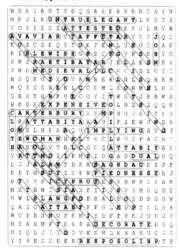

Cat Facts, puzzle 142

Cat Facts, puzzle 143

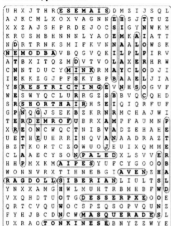

Cat Facts, puzzle 144

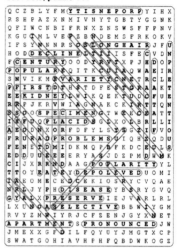

Cat Facts, puzzle 145

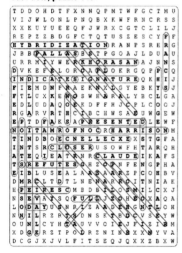

Cat Facts, puzzle 146

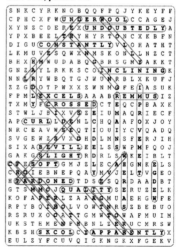

Cat Facts, puzzle 147

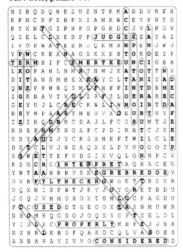

Cat Facts, puzzle 148

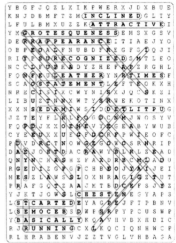

Cat Facts, puzzle 149

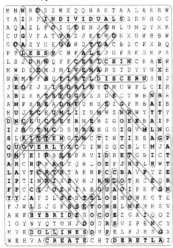

Cat Facts, puzzle 150

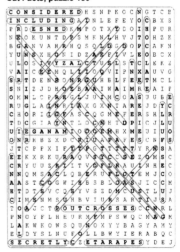

American Shorthair, References

1. ^ Stephens, Gloria; Yamazaki, Tetsu (2001). *Legacy of the Cat* (2nd ed.). San Francisco: Chronicle Books. p. 49. ISBN 0-8118-2910-3.
2. ^ "Top 10 Most Popular Breeds". The Cat Fanciers' Association. Retrieved 2012-05-21.
3. "American Shorthair Breed". The International Cat Association (TICA). 2012. Retrieved 2012-05-21.
4. Cat Fanciers' Association American Shorthair breed profile
5. http://en.wikipedia.org/wiki/American_Shorthair

Kitten, References

1. "Kitten". *Oxford English Dictionary* (3rd ed.). Oxford University Press. September 2005.
2. ^ Tsutsui, Toshihiko; Stabenfeldt, George H. (1993). "Biology of ovarian cycles, pregnancy and pseudopregnancy in the domestic cat". *Journal of Reproduction and Fertility Supplement* 47: 29–35. PMID 8229938.
3. ^ Miglino, Maria Angelica; Ambrósio, Carlos Eduardo; dos Santos Martins, Daniele; Wenceslau, Cristiane Valverde; Pfarrer, Christiane; Leiser, Rudolf (2006). "The carnivore pregnancy: the development of the embryo and fetal membranes". *Theriogenology* 66 (6–7): 1699–702. doi:10.1016/j.theriogenology.2006.02.027. PMID 16563485.
4. Foster, Race. "How to Raise Orphan Kittens". *Pet Education: Expert information for all types of pets*. Retrieved 2011-03-07.
5. ^ Casal, Margret L.; Jezyk, Peter F.; Giger, Urs (1996). "Transfer of colostral antibodies from queens to their kittens". *American Journal of Veterinary Research* 57 (11): 1653–8. PMID 8915447.
6. ^ Sturgess, Kit; Hurley, Karyl J. (2005). "Nutrition and Welfare". In Rochlitz, Irene. *Animal Welfare Volume 3: The Welfare of Cats*. p. 243. doi:10.1007/1-4020-3227-7_9.
7. ^ Tootle, John S.; Friedlander, Michael J. (1989). "Postnatal development of the spatial contrast sensitivity of X- and Y-cells in the kitten retinogeniculate pathway". *Journal of Neuroscience* 9 (4): 1325–40. PMID 2703879.
8. ^ Poirier, Frank E.; Hussey, L. Kaye (1982). "Nonhuman Primate Learning: The Importance of Learning from an Evolutionary Perspective". *Anthropology & Education Quarterly* 13 (2): 133–148. doi:10.1525/aeq.1982.13.2.05x1830j. JSTOR 3216627.
9. ^ Sturgess, Kit; Hurley, Karyl J. (2005). "Nutrition and Welfare". In Rochlitz, Irene. *Animal Welfare Volume 3: The Welfare of Cats*. p. 244. doi:10.1007/1-4020-3227-7_9.
10. Crowell-Davis, Sharon L. (2005). "Cat Behaviour. Social Organization, Communication and Development". In Rochlitz, Irene. *Animal Welfare Volume 3: The Welfare of Cats*. p. 18.doi:10.1007/1-4020-3227-7_1.
11. ^ Sunquist, Mel; Sunquist, Fiona (2002). *Wild Cats of the World*. University of Chicago Press. ISBN 0-226-77999-8.
12. ^ Olson, Patricia N.; Kustritz, Margaret V.; Johnston, Shirley D. (2001). "Early-age neutering of dogs and cats in the United States (a review)". *Journal of Reproduction and Fertility Supplement* 57: 223–232. PMID 11787153.
13. ^ Spain, C. Victor; Scarlett, Janet M.; Houpt, Katherine A. (2004). "Long-term risks and benefits of early-age gonadectomy in cats". *Journal of the American Veterinary Medical Association* 224 (3): 372–379. doi:10.2460/javma.2004.224.372. PMID 14765796.
14. ^ Rogers, Quinton R.; Morris, James G. (1979). "Essentiality of amino acids for the growing kitten". *Journal of Nutrition* 109 (4): 718–723. PMID 430271.
15. ^ Guilford, W. Grant (1994). "Nutritional management of gastrointestinal tract diseases of dogs and cats". *Journal of Nutrition* 124 (12 (Supplement)): 2663S–2669S. PMID 7996263.
16. ^ Heath, Sarah E. (2005). "Behaviour Problems and Welfare". In Rochlitz, Irene. *Animal Welfare Volume 3: The Welfare of Cats*. p. 102. doi:10.1007/1-4020-3227-7_4.
17. http://en.wikipedia.org/wiki/Kitten

Arabian Mau, References

1. ^Au, Jessica (October 27, 2008). "UAE's 'Desert Cats' Recognised as Breed". *The National* (UAE: Abu Dhabi Media). Archived from the original on January 3, 2013. Retrieved January 3, 2013.
2. ^ Arabian Mau, WCF

3. ^ "Arabian Mau Cats 101". Animal Planet.

4. http://en.wikipedia.org/wiki/Arabian_Mau

Cat Anatomy, References

1. ^ "At Home: Care / Health: Understanding Cats". Archived from the original on 1 February 2008. Retrieved 15 August 2005.

2. ^ Syufy F. "The Nose Knows Cats' Amazing Sense of Scent". *About.com*.

3. ^ "Cat Anatomy". *cat-chitchat.pictures-of-cats.org*. 9 July 2008.

4. ^ Lacquaniti, F.; Grasso, R.; Zago, M. (1 August 1999)."Motor Patterns in Walking". *News Physiol. Sci.* **14** (4): 168–174. PMID 11390844.

5. ^ Christensen, Wendy (2004). *Outwitting Cats*. Globe Pequot. p. 23. ISBN 1-59228-240-7.

6. ^ Armes, Annetta F. (22 December 1900). "Outline of Cat Lessons". *The School Journal* **LXI**: 659. Retrieved 12 November 2007.

7. ^ Danforth, C. H. (1947). "Heredity of Polydactyly in the Cat". *Journal of Heredity* **38** (4): 107–112.PMID 20242531.

8. ^ "Normal Values For Dog and Cat Temperature, Blood Tests, Urine and other information in ThePetCenter.com". Retrieved 1 August 2005.

9. ^ Cat Health And Cat Metabolism Information For The Best Cat Care. Highlander Pet Center

10. ^ "Vaccinate Your Cat at Home". Retrieved 18 October 2006.

11. ^ Kellman, Rich. "The Cat Comes Back". Retrieved 1 March 2010.[*dead link*]

12. ^ "How to Give Subcutaneous Fluids to a Cat".*wikihow.com*. Retrieved 18 October 2006.

13. ^ "Scruffing your dog or cat". *pets.c*. Retrieved 26 February 2008.

14. ^ Gillis, Rick (ed.) (22 July 2002). "Cat Skeleton". *Zoolab: A Website for Animal Biology*. La Crosse, WI: University of Wisconsin. Archived from the original on 6 December 2006. Retrieved 7 September 2012.

15. ^ Case, Linda P. (2003). *The Cat: Its Behavior, Nutrition, and Health*. Ames, IA: Iowa State University Press. ISBN 0-8138-0331-4.

16. ^ Smith, Patricia; Tchernov, Eitan (1992). *Structure, Function and Evolution of teeth*. Freund Publishing House Ltd. p. 217. ISBN 965-222-270-4.

17. ^ Rosenzweig, L. J. (1990). *Anatomy of the Cat: Text and Dissection Guide*. Wm. C. Brown Publishers Dubuque, IA. p. 110, ISBN 0697055795.

18. ^ *a b* The cat's genital system and reproduction. aniwa.com

19. http://en.wikipedia.org/wiki/Cat_anatomy

British Shorthair, References

1. ^ "British Shorthair Breed Profile". TheCatSite. Retrieved 2006-08-31.

2. ^ "Analysis of Breeds Registered by the GCCF". Governing Council of the Cat Fancy. Retrieved 2008-01-01.

3. ^ *a b c* "British Shorthair: Cat Breed FAQ". Cat Fanciers. Retrieved 2006-07-28.

4. ^ *a b* "British Shorthair Cat Breed Information and Pictures". PussCats.com. Retrieved 2006-09-08.[*dead link*]

5. ^ "British Blue Cat Physical Characteristics". Retrieved 2009-11-10.

6. ^ "Breed Standard: British Shorthair" (PDF). Cat Fanciers' Association. Retrieved 2011-08-14.

7. ^ http://www.findakitten.co.uk/bsh.html "British Shorthair Personality"

8. ^ http://www.ncbi.nlm.nih.gov/pubmed/21736622

9. ^ "Polycystic Kidney Disease". *Genetic welfare problems of companion animals*. Universities Federation for Animal Welfare. Retrieved 4 August 2012.

10. ^ http://www.ncbi.nlm.nih.gov/pubmed/18060738

11. http://en.wikipedia.org/wiki/British_Shorthair

Abyssinian Cat, References

1. ^ "Abyssinian Profile", Catz Inc., accessed 4 Oct 2009

2. ^ Cat Fanciers' Association. "Breed Profile: Abyssinian". 2011.

3. ^ *a b* Pollard, Michael. *The Encyclopedia of the Cat*. United Kingdom: Parragon Publishing, 1999.

4. ^ Highfield, Roger (2007-10-31). "Cinnamon the cat could offer hope to the blind". The Daily Telegraph. Retrieved 2007-11-01.

5. ^ "TICA page of Abyssinian Breed". TICA. Retrieved 2012-05-21.

6. http://en.wikipedia.org/wiki/Abyssinian_(cat)

Feral Cat, References

1. ^ Holton, Louise (June 2007). "Wild Things? An Introduction To Feral Cats". Bandaras News. Retrieved 21 November 2010.

2. ^ "Feral and unwanted cats". *gw.govt.nz*. August 2006.

3. ^ *a b c* Morelle, Rebecca (29 January 2013). "Cats killing billions of animals in the US". *BBC News*. Retrieved 12 February 2013.

4. ^ *a b* Feral Cat Coalition / Ray Savage (November 2009)."Taming Feral Kittens".

5. ^ "Cat Behavior 101 – Everything you Need to Know About Cat Behavior". Cats.about.com. 19 November 2011. Retrieved 10 December 2011.

6. ^ "How to Turn a Stray Cat Into a Pet – Page 1". Petplace.com. Retrieved 10 December 2011.

7. ^ Levy JK, Gale DW, Gale LA, JK (2003). "Evaluation of the effect of a long-term trap-neuter-return and adoption program on a free-roaming cat population" (PDF). *J. Am. Vet. Med. Assoc.* 222 (1): 42–6.doi:10.2460/javma.2003.222.42. PMID 12523478.

8. ^ Foley, P.; Foley, J. E.; Levy, J. K.; Paik, T. (2005). "Analysis of the impact of trap-neuter-return programs on populations of feral cats". *Journal of the American Veterinary Medical Association* 227 (11): 1775–1781.doi:10.2460/javma.2005.227.1775.PMID 16342526. edit

9. ^ E. J. Taylor, C. Adams & R. Neville (1995). "Some nutritional aspects of ageing in dogs and cats".*Proceedings of the Nutrition Society* 54 (3): 645–656.doi:10.1079/PNS19950064. PMID 8643702.

10. ^ Abbott, Ian; Department of Environment and Conservation (2008). "Origin and spread of the cat, Felis catus, on mainland Australia: re-examination of the current conceptual model with additional information".*Conservation Science Western Australia Journal* (7). Retrieved 11 February 2013.

11. ^ Dickman, Chris (May 1996). *Overview of the Impacts of Feral Cats on Australian Native Fauna.* The Director of National Parks and Wildlife – Australian Nature Conservation Agency – Institute of Wildlife Research.ISBN 0-642-21379-8. Retrieved 11 February 2013.

12. ^ Cat diet on Macaronesia (Atlantic Ocean). petsaspests.blogspot.com.es (28 March 2013).

13. ^ Forbush, Edward Howe (1916). The Domestic Cat: Bird Killer, Mouser and Destroyer of Wildlife, Boston, Wright & Potter printing co.

14. ^ Rothschild, Walter (1905). Extinct Birds, London : Hutchinson.

15. ^ Collar, N. J. (2001). *Endangered Birds* 2. New York: Academic Press. p. 400. in *Encyclopedia of Biodiversity*

16. ^ The Threat Of FeralCats. Environment.nsw.gov.au (28 October 2011). Retrieved on 5 May 2013.

17. ^ "Interactions between feral cats, foxes, native carnivores, and rabbits in Australia". *CSIRO Sustainable Ecosystems / Arthur Rylah Institute for Environmental Research.* Sep 2004. Retrieved 12 February 2013.

18. ^ King, Carolyn (1984) *Immigrant Killers.* Auckland: Oxford University Press. ISBN 0-19-558121-0

19. ^ "Toxic bait and baiting strategies for feral cats". University of Nebraska – Lincoln: Proceedings of the Fifteenth Vertebrate Pest Conference 1992. 1992.

20. ^ *a b* Moors, P.J.; Atkinson, I.A.E. (1984). "Predation on seabirds by introduced animals, and factors affecting its severity" in *Status and Conservation of the World's Seabirds*. Cambridge: ICBP. ISBN 0-946888-03-5.

21. ^ Barcott, Bruce (2 December 2007). "Kill the Cat That Kills the Bird?". *The New York Times*.

22. ^ Pontier, D.; L. Say, F. Debias, J. Bried, J. Thioulouse, T. Micol & E. Natoli (2002). *The diet of feral cats (Felis catus L.) at five sites on the Grande Terre, Kerguelen archipelago*. doi:10.1007/s00300-002-0424-5.

23. ^ Nogales, Manuel; Martin, Aurelio; Tershy, Bernie R.; Donlan, C. Josh; Veitch, Dick; Puerta, Nestor; Wood, Bill; Alonso, Jesus (2004). "A review of feral cat eradication on islands". *Conservation Biology* 18 (2): 310.doi:10.1111/j.1523-1739.2004.00442.x.

24. ^ Stamps celebrate seabird return. Birdlife.org (27 July 2005). Retrieved on 5 May 2013.

25. ^ "Up against rats, rabbits and costs". *The Sydney Morning Herald*. 12 April 2007.

26. ^ Fears for sub-antarctic island plagued by rabbits. ABC News (15 July 2006).

27. ^ Draper, Michelle and La Canna, Xavier (14 January 2009)Cat kill devastates Macquarie Island. Nine News

28. ^ Macquarie Island World Heritage Area. Plan for the Eradication of Rabbits and Rodents on Macquarie Island. Parks and Wildlife Service, Tasmania. parks.tas.gov.au

29. ^ Driscoll, C. A.; Menotti-Raymond, M.; Roca, A. L.; Hupe, K.; Johnson, W. E.; Geffen, E.; Harley, E. H.; Delibes, M. et al. (2007). "The Near Eastern Origin of Cat Domestication".*Science* 317 (5837): 519–523.doi:10.1126/science.1139518. PMID 17600185. edit

30. ^ European wildcat (*Felis silvestris grampia*) Arkive.org

31. ^ European wildcat species account IUCN Species Survival Commission. *See also Genetic pollution)*Cat Specialist Group

32. ^ Genetic diversity and introgression in the Scottish wildcat. *Molecular Ecology* (2001) 10: 319–336.

33. ^ The Encyclopedia of Mammals, OUP, ISBN 978-0-19-920608-7, pages 656–657

34. ^ "CDC – Toxoplasmosis". Cdc.gov. 2 November 2010. Retrieved 10 December 2011.

35. ^ "Frequently Asked Questions". saveacat.org. Retrieved 21 November 2010.

36. ^ Levy, J. K.; Gale, D. W.; Gale, L. A. (2003). "Evaluation of the effect of a long-term trap-neuter-return and adoption program on a free-roaming cat population". *Journal of the American Veterinary Medical Association* 222 (1): 42–46.doi:10.2460/javma.2003.222.42. PMID 12523478. edit

37. ^ Hughes, K. L.; Slater, M. R. (2002). "Implementation of a Feral Cat Management Program on a University Campus".*Journal of Applied Animal Welfare Science* 5 (1): 15–28.doi:10.1207/S15327604JAWS0501_2.PMID 12738586. edit

38. ^ Zaunbrecher, K. I.; Smith, R. E. (1993). "Neutering of feral cats as an alternative to eradication programs". *Journal of the American Veterinary Medical Association* 203 (3): 449–452. PMID 8226225. edit

39. ^ Castillo, D., and A. L. Clarke (2003). "Trap/neuter/release methods ineffective in controlling domestic cat "colonies" on public lands". *Natural Areas Journal* 23: 247–253.

40. ^ Hamilton, Frank RE· 'The Truth About Trap-Neuter-Return and Feral Cat Colony Movement'. floridacatnews.com

41. ^ Mitchell, Carolyn (January 2000). "Femmes Ferals!". Best Friends Magazine. p. 12. Retrieved 21 November 2010. (PDF)

42. ^ "Cat Action Network-List of Participating Rescue Groups and Animal Shelters-TNR". Alley Cat Rescue. Retrieved 21 November 2010.

43. ^ "Feral Cat Organizations". Humane Society of the United States. 21 October 2009.

44. ^ "Position On Trap-Neuter-Return (TNR)". Humane Society of the United States. Retrieved 21 November 2010.

45. ^ "Taking A Broader View Of Cats In The Community". Animal Sheltering. September–October 2008. Retrieved 21 November 2010.

46. ^ Kozaryn, Linda D. "Cat Herding on the Military Range-"Trap, Neuter, Return," Cat Lovers Urge". United States Department of Defense. Retrieved 21 November 2010.

47. ^ Kozaryn, Linda D. "Cat Herding on the Military Range-DoD Advocates Humane Cat Control". United States Department of Defense. Retrieved 21 November 2010.

48. ^ Berthier, K.; Langlais, M.; Auger, P.; Pontier, D. (2000)."Dynamics of a feline virus with two transmission modes within exponentially growing host populations".*Proceedings of the Royal Society B: Biological Sciences*267 (1457): 2049–2056. doi:10.1098/rspb.2000.1248.PMC 1690787. PMID 11416908. edit

49. ^ a b c d Ratcliffe, Norman; Bell, Jim; Pelembe, Tara; Boyle, Dave; Banjamin, Raymond; White, Richard; Godley, Brenda; Stevenson, Jim et al. (2009). "The eradication of feral cats from Ascension Island and its subsequent recolonization by seabirds". *Oryx* 44 (1): 20–29.doi:10.1017/S003060530999069X.

50. ^ Hamilton, Jill (30 July 2007). "Blair and the stray cats of Jerusalem". *JPost.com*. Retrieved 25 August 2009.

51. http://en.wikipedia.org/wiki/Feral_cat

Cat Communication, References

1. ^ D. S. Mills, Current issues and research in veterinary behavioral medicine: papers, Purdue University Press, Image at Books.google.com
2. ^ Dennis C. Turner, Paul Patrick Gordon Bateson, Patrick Bateson, *The domestic cat: the biology of its behaviour*, Cambridge University Press, p. 68 Image at Books.google.com
3. ^ *a b* "Meowing and Yowling". *Virtual Pet Behaviorist*. ASPCA. Retrieved 28 May 2012.
4. ^ "νιαουρίζω". *Word Reference* (in Greek). WordReference.com. Retrieved 28 May 2012.
5. ^ Peggy Bivens (2002). *Language Arts 1, Volume 1*. Saddleback Publishing. p. 59. ISBN 978-1-562-54508-6.
6. ^ Schötz, Susanne (May 30 – June 1, 2012). "A phonetic pilot study of vocalizations in three cats" (PDF). Proceedings Fonetik 2012. The XXVth Swedish Phonetics conference. University of Gothenburg. pp. 45–58.
7. ^ "caterwaul". *Dictionary.com*. Dictionary.com, LLC. Retrieved 28 May 2012.
8. ^ Dennis C. Turner, Patrick Bateson (eds.) (2000). *The domestic cat: the biology of its behaviour*. Cambridge University Press. pp. 71, 72, 86 and 88. ISBN 978-0521-63648-3. Retrieved 3 January 2012.
9. ^ "Why and how do cats purr?". Library of Congress. Retrieved 10 April 2011.
10. ^ K.M. Dyce, W.O. Sack and C.J.G. Wensing in *Textbook of Veterinary Anatomy 3rd Ed*. 2002, Saunders, Philadelphia; p156
11. ^ How A Puma Purrs
12. ^ "An acoustic analysis of purring in the cheetah (*Acinonyx jubatus*) and in the domestic cat (*Felis catus*)". *Proceedings from Fonetik 2011*. Retrieved 2012-09-02.
13. ^ "A comparative acoustic analysis of purring in four cats". *Proceedings from Fonetik 2011*. Retrieved 2012-09-02.
14. ^ "A comparative acoustic analysis of purring in four cheetahs". *Proceedings from Fonetik 2011*. Retrieved 2012-09-02.
15. ^ Breton, R. Roger; Creek, Nancy J. "Overview of Felidae". Cougar Hill Web. Retrieved May 23, 2013.
16. ^ Helgren, J. Anne (1999). *Communicating with Your Cat*. Barron's Educational Series. ISBN 0-7641-0855-7.
17. ^ Cat articles on Iams website
18. ^ "Common Cat Behaviors". *Best Cat Tips*. http://www.best-cat-tips.com. Retrieved 28 May 2012.
19. ^ Mary White. "Cat Behavior Tips". *LifeTips*. LifeTips. Retrieved 28 May 2012.
20. ^ "Cat bites, infection risk 'are no joke'," Deseret Morning News Tuesday, Dec. 6, 2005
21. ^ "Play Therapy Pt. 2," Cats International retrieved May 22, 2007
22. ^ Dennis C. Turner; Patrick Bateman, eds. (2000). *The Domestic Cat* (2nd ed.). University Press, Cambridge. pp. 69–70. ISBN 0521636485. Retrieved 28 May 2012.
23. ^ Bailey, Dr. Steven (2011-10-02). "Butting heads with your cats". *felinedocs.com*. Retrieved 2013-03-27.
24. http://en.wikipedia.org/wiki/Cat_communication

Chartreux, References

1. ^ http://www.loof.asso.fr/gp/lettre_annee.php
2. ^ **(French)** DR Rousselet-Blanc. "Le chat". p. 160. ISBN 2035174023. Unknown parameter |chap= ignored (help); Unknown parameter |éditeur=ignored (help); Unknown parameter |année= ignored (help); Unknown parameter | langue= ignored (help);
3. ^ **(English)** "Magdaleine Pinceloup de la Grange, née de Parseval". *http://www.getty.edu/*. Retrieved 5 août 2009. Unknown parameter |éditeur=ignored (help)
4. http://en.wikipedia.org/wiki/Chartreux

Fogle, Bruce (2001). *The New Encyclopedia of the Cat*. New York: DK Publishing Inc [Dorling Kindersley]. ISBN 0-7894-8021-2.

Siegal, Mordecai (1997). The breeds. Chapter 2 in *The Cornell Book of Cats: A Comprehensive and Authoritative Medical Reference for Every Cat and Kitten*. Second edition. Edited by Mordecai Siegal. Villard:New York. ISBN 978-0-679-44953-9.

Simonnet, Jean (1990). *The Chartreux Cat*. Translated by Jerome M. Auerbach. Paris: Synchro Company. ISBN 978-2-

9506009-0-5. (This book's ISBNdb.com page lists "Auerbach Pub" as the publisher, but the book itself gives "Synchro Company, Paris" on an unnumbered page immediately following page 190.)

Helgren, J. Anne (1997). *Encyclopedia of Cat Breeds*. Barron's Educational Series. ISBN 978-0-7641-5067-8.

Cat Health, References

1. ^ Bites, puncture wounds, and abscesses, John A. Bukowski, DVM, MPH, PhD and Susan E. Aiello, DVM, ELS, WebVet.com; accessed March 30, 2009.
2. ^ Rabies surveillance in the United States during 2006.
3. ^ Welcome to Healthypet com!
4. ^ Zoonotic Disease: What Can I Catch From My Cat?
5. ^ Vegetarian dogs and cats: Kibble doesn't cut it anymore
6. ^ Nutrition for Cats
7. ^ Verlinden, A.; Hesta, M., Millet, S., Janssens, G.P. (4-5 2006). "Food Allergy in Dogs and Cats: A Review". *Critical Reviews in Food Science and Nutrition (Taylor & Francis)* **46** (3): 259–273.doi:10.1080/10408390591001117. PMID 16527756.
8. ^ John E. Bauer, D.V.M., Ph.D., Dipl. A.C.V.N. (2005-01-01). "Nutritional Requirements and Related Diseases". *The Merck Veterinary Manual, 9th edition. ISBN 0-911910-50-6*. Merck & Co., Inc.Retrieved 2006-10-27.
9. ^ "A Poison Safe Home". *Animal Poison Control Center*. American Society for the Prevention of Cruelty to Animals (ASPCA). Retrieved 2012-07-08.
10. ^ "Toxic and Non-Toxic Plants". *Animal Poison Control Center*. American Society for the Prevention of Cruelty to Animals (ASPCA). Retrieved 2012-07-08.
11. ^ "Human Medications and Cosmetics". *Animal Poison Control Center*. American Society for the Prevention of Cruelty to Animals (ASPCA). Retrieved 2012-07-08.
12. ^ "Cleaning Products". *Animal Poison Control Center*. American Society for the Prevention of Cruelty to Animals (ASPCA). Retrieved 2012-07-08.
13. ^ "People Foods". *Animal Poison Control Center*. American Society for the Prevention of Cruelty to Animals (ASPCA). Retrieved 2012-07-08.
14. ^ "Plants and Your Cat". The Cat Fanciers' Association, Inc. Retrieved 2007-05-15.
15. ^ Allen AL (2003). "The diagnosis of acetaminophen toxicosis in a cat". *Can Vet J* **44** (6): 509–10. PMC 340185. PMID 12839249.
16. ^ *a b c d* "Toxic to Cats". Vetinfo4Cats. Retrieved 2007-01-18.
17. ^ Camille DeClementi; Keith L. Bailey, Spencer C. Goldstein, and Michael Scott Orser (December 2004). "Suspected toxicosis after topical administration of minoxidil in 2 cats". *Journal of Veterinary Emergency and Critical Care* **14** (4): 287–292. doi:10.1111/j.1476-4431.2004.04014.x.
18. ^ "Minoxidil Warning". ShowCatsOnline.com. Archived from the original on 2007-01-03. Retrieved 2007-01-18. "Very small amounts of Minoxidil can result [in] serious problems or death"
19. ^ Rousseaux CG, Smith RA, Nicholson S (1986). "Acute Pinesol toxicity in a domestic cat". *Vet Hum Toxicol* **28** (4): 316–7. PMID 3750813.
20. ^ "Antifreeze Warning". The Cat Fanciers' Association, Inc. Retrieved 2007-05-15.
21. ^ K. Bischoff, F. Guale (1998). "Australian tea tree (Melaleuca alternifolia) Oil Poisoning in three purebred cats" (– Scholar search). *Journal of Veterinary Diagnostic Investigation* **10** (108). Archived from the original on October 15, 2006. Retrieved 2006-10-17.[*dead link*]
22. ^ TEA TREE OIL - TOXIC TO CATS
23. ^ Be Wary of Aromatherapy Claims for Cats
24. http://en.wikipedia.org/wiki/Cat_health

Tabby Cat, References

1. ^A Tribute to Tabby Cats in all Their Manifestations. About.com:Cats. Retrieved on January 31, 2008

2. ^ Cat Colors FAQ Cat Fanciers. Retrieved on January 31, 2008
3. ^ "Glossary of Cat Terms". Retrieved 24 November 2009.
4. ^ Cats of a Different Color, Agouti.
5. ^ ataviar - Definición - WordReference.com. Retrieved on May 6th, 2013
6. ^ Online Etymology Dictionary
7. ^ Oliver Lawson Dick, ed. *Aubrey's Brief Lives. Edited from the Original Manuscripts*, 1949, p. Xxxvi.
8. http://en.wikipedia.org/wiki/Tabby

Point Coloration, References

1. ^ D. L. Imes *et al.* (April 2006). "Albinism in the domestic cat (*Felis catus*) is associated with a *tyrosinase* (*TYR*) mutation" (Short Communication). *Animal Genetics* **37** (2): 175.doi:10.1111/j.1365-2052.2005.01409.x. PMC 1464423. PMID 16573534. Retrieved 2006-05-29.
2. http://en.wikipedia.org/wiki/Point_(coat_color)

Persian Cat, References

1. ^ *a b c* Hartwell, Sarah. Longhaired Cats. Messybeast.com
2. ^ *a b c* Helgren, J. Anne.(2006) Iams Cat Breed Guide: Persian Cats Telemark Productions
3. ^ The Ascent of Cat Breeds: Genetic Evaluations of Breeds and Worldwide Random Bred Populations Genomics. 2008 January; 91(1): 12–21.
4. ^ Weir, Harrison. (1889) Our Cats and All About Them
5. ^ Simpson, Frances. (1903) The Book of the Cat
6. ^ *a b* Champion, Dorothy Bevill (1909). *Everybody's Cat Book*. New York: Lent & Graff. p. 17.
7. ^ Solid Color Persians Are. .Solid As A Rock? Cat Fanciers' Almanac, November 2002
8. ^ Stargazing: A Historical View of Solid Color Persians Cat Fanciers' Almanac. March 1995
9. ^ *a b c* Hartwell, Sarah. Novelty Breeds and Ultra-Cats - A Breed Too Far? Messybeast
10. ^ "2003 Breed Council Ballot Proposals and Results". CFA Persian Breed Council. 2004. Retrieved 2009-10-17.
11. ^ "2006 Breed Council Ballot Proposals and Results". CFA Persian Breed Council. 2007. Retrieved 2009-10-17.
12. ^ Bi-Color and Calico Persians: Past, Present and Future Cat Fanciers' Almanac. May 1998
13. ^ Persian Self Breed Standard Governing Council of the Cat Fancy
14. ^ Helgren. J. Anne. (2006) Iams Breed Profile: Himalayan Telemark Productions.
15. ^ Himalayan-Persian Cat Fanciers' Almanac May 1999
16. ^ Breed Profile: Persian - Solid Color Division Cat Fanciers' Association
17. ^ CFA ANNUAL AND EXECUTIVE BOARD MEETINGS JUNE 23-27, 2004
18. ^ Helgren, J. Anne.(2006) Iams Cat Breed Guide. Exotic Shorthair Telemark Productions
19. ^ Hartwell, Sarah Dwarf, Midget and Miniature Cats -- Purebreds

Enjoy all of the

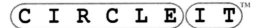

Word Search
Puzzle Books

from

LowryGlobalMedia.com

Short Stories Series:

Circle It, Snapshots, Word Search, Puzzle Book (ISBN 978-1-938625-17-6)

Circle It, Moments, Word Search, Puzzle Book (ISBN 978-1-938625-16-9)

Circle It, Anecdotes, Word Search, Puzzle Book (ISBN 978-1-938625-23-7)

Circle It, Snippets, Word Search, Puzzle Book (ISBN 978-1-938625-41-1)

Facts Series:

Circle It, Dog Facts, Book 1, Word Search, Puzzle Book (ISBN 978-1-938625-21-3)

Circle It, Cat Facts, Book 2, Word Search, Puzzle Book (ISBN 978-1-938625-25-1)

Circle It, Elk Moose & Deer Facts, Word Search, Puzzle Book (ISBN 978-1-938625-35-0)

Circle It, Bald Eagle Facts, Word Search, Puzzle Book (ISBN 978-1-938625-39-8)

Circle It, Jimmy Fallon Facts, Word Search, Puzzle Book (ISBN 978-1-938625-30-5)

Circle It, Coyote and Wolf Facts, Word Search, Puzzle Book (ISBN 978-1-938625-33-6)

Circle It, Bear Facts, Word Search, Puzzle Book (ISBN 978-1-938625-32-9)

Circle It, Trout Facts, Word Search, Puzzle Book (ISBN 978-1-938625-38-1)

Circle It, Italian Coffee Facts, Word Search, Puzzle Book (ISBN 978-1-938625-18-3)

...and many more, all available from your favorite retailer or online book seller.

Check LowryGlobalMedia.com for the latest releases!

CPSIA information can be obtained
at www.ICGtesting.com
Printed in the USA
FFOW03n0336140517
35442FF